"Kim Meeder vibrantly shares—and lives—an amazing story of hope and restoration. A triumph of recovery for wounded hearts!"

—Louie Giglio
Director, Passion Conferences, bestselling author

"Kim Meeder proves that even in our fallen world, hope is not lost. Despite horrific pasts and deep pain, God's mercy is shown true as wounds are healed and hope is restored."

—Mike Yankoski
Author, *Under the Overpass*

"As in her debut book, *Hope Rising*, Kim Meeder again shares with us the blessings of hope fulfilled. In *Bridge Called Hope*, Kim uses her inimitable gift of communicating to transport us to the world of Crystal Peaks Youth Ranch—a place where the flames of hope are reignited, broken lives find healing, and mountains are moved. Stirring, encouraging, and inspirational, *Bridge Called Hope* reminds us that hope is heaven sent for everyone, and that we, too, can make a positive difference in others' lives."

—Eric Close
Actor

# BRIDGE CALLED
# HOPE

## KIM MEEDER

Multnomah Books

BRIDGE CALLED HOPE
published by Multnomah Books
© 2006 by Kim Meeder

International Standard Book Number: 978-1-59052-655-2

Cover photograph by JWH Design Services
Interior design and typset by Katherine Lloyd, Sisters, OR

Published in the United States by WaterBrook Multnomah, an
imprint of the Crown Publishing Group, a division of Random
House Inc., New York.

Multnomah and its mountain colophon are registered trademarks of
Random House Inc.

Printed in the United States of America

For information:
MULTNOMAH BOOKS
12265 ORACLE BOULEVARD, SUITE 200
COLORADO SPRINGS, CO 80921

Library of Congress Cataloging-in-Publication Data

Meeder, Kim.

Bridge called hope / Kim Meeder.

p. cm.

ISBN 1-59052-655-4

1. Crystal Peaks Youth Ranch (Bend, Or.) 2. Problem youth-
-Services for--Oregon. 3. Horses--Therapeutic use. 4. Animal
rescue--Oregon. I. Title.

HV1435.O7M436 2006

362.74'85--dc22

2006022794

10 11—10 9 8 7 6

FOR TROY

*Welcome home, my Prince.*

Hope is like a
sky full of
stars…whether
we see them or
not doesn't
change the fact
that they are
always there.
Truly, it is not
until the night is
at its very
darkest…that
we see them
shine the most
clearly.

# Contents

*In Appreciation* . . . . . . . . . . . . . . . . . . . . . . . . . . . . . . . . . . . .9

*About the Ranch* . . . . . . . . . . . . . . . . . . . . . . . . . . . . . . . . . . . .11

*Hope Is* . . . . . . . . . . . . . . . . . . . . . . . . . . . . . . . . . . . . . . . . . . .13

1 Proof . . . . . . . . . . . . . . . . . . . . . . . . . . . . . . . . . . . . . . . . 15

2 Side by Side . . . . . . . . . . . . . . . . . . . . . . . . . . . . . . . . . . 26

3 Bright Spot . . . . . . . . . . . . . . . . . . . . . . . . . . . . . . . . . . 38

4 Littlest Bear . . . . . . . . . . . . . . . . . . . . . . . . . . . . . . . . . . 44

5 Promise Land . . . . . . . . . . . . . . . . . . . . . . . . . . . . . . . . 57

6 Full Circle . . . . . . . . . . . . . . . . . . . . . . . . . . . . . . . . . . . 69

7 Fruits and Vegetables . . . . . . . . . . . . . . . . . . . . . . . . . 81

8 Simply...Step Up . . . . . . . . . . . . . . . . . . . . . . . . . . . . . 82

9 Phoenix . . . . . . . . . . . . . . . . . . . . . . . . . . . . . . . . . . . . 103

10 Love Matters . . . . . . . . . . . . . . . . . . . . . . . . . . . . . . . . 129

11 The Prescription . . . . . . . . . . . . . . . . . . . . . . . . . . . . . 139

12 Cleansing Fire . . . . . . . . . . . . . . . . . . . . . . . . . . . . . . . 142

13 Perspective . . . . . . . . . . . . . . . . . . . . . . . . . . . . . . . . . . 154

14 A Dog's Tale . . . . . . . . . . . . . . . . . . . . . . . . . . . . . . . . 161

15 May Day . . . . . . . . . . . . . . . . . . . . . . . . . . . . . . . . . . . 173

16 Bruises . . . . . . . . . . . . . . . . . . . . . . . . . . . . . . . . . . . . . 177

17 Horse with Spots (Part 1) . . . . . . . . . . . . . . . . . . . . . 185

18 Horse with Spots (Part 2) . . . . . . . . . . . . . . . . . . . . . 190

19 Horse with Spots (Part 3) . . . . . . . . . . . . . . . . . . . . . 199

20 Friendship . . . . . . . . . . . . . . . . . . . . . . . . . . . . . . . . . . 210

21 Hannah's Legacy . . . . . . . . . . . . . . . . . . . . . . . . . . . . . 222

22 Coming Home . . . . . . . . . . . . . . . . . . . . . . . . . . . . . . . 233

*Epilogue:* Bridge Called Hope . . . . . . . . . . . . . . . . . . . . . 239

Bridge "Crossings" . . . . . . . . . . . . . . . . . . . . . . . . . . . . . . 243

My Friend, you're the best, you're our foundation, you're our strength, you're our friend, you're our family, you're our legacy, you're our cheerleader, you're our shoulder, you're our mirror, you're our voice in the stillness, you're our light in the darkness, you're our salt, you're our truth, you're our sidekick, you're our encouragement, you're our voice of reason, you're our financial help, you're our hammer and nails, you're our hug, you're our hay in the barn, you're our pennies from heaven, you're our tears of joy, you're our vitamin M, you're our hot mocha joe, you're our ear, you're our callused hands, you're our prayer partner, you're our smile, you're our starry night, you're our campfire, you're our heartbeat, you're our hands and feet, you're our stone, you're our reflection, you're our joy, you're our mortar, you're our carpenter, you're our voice across the ocean, you're our warrior, you're our laughter, you're our sticky kiss, you're our balance, you're our trainer, you're our hope, you're our rest, you're our hide-and-seeker, you're our bright spot, you're our ripple effect, you're our student, you're our kiwi, you're our rescuer, you're our cleansing fire, you're our step up, you're our flowers, you're our promise, you're our wisdom, you're our hope...you're our hero.

# *In Appreciation*

To say a simple thank-you to everyone who has shouldered with us, believed with us, and sacrificed with us to see the ranch and this book go forward…feels a bit like giving a raindrop to represent the ocean. Know that I am moved by you, every one of you, and continue to be overwhelmingly grateful that you are all part of my life.

For our extended family of friends throughout this great nation and beyond, know that every card, e-mail, letter, and gift, from each individual, has become a cherished part of what this ranch is becoming. You bless me.

For Thomas, your wisdom is my sharpening stone. You inspire me to grow.

For the ranch staff, your every act of selflessness holds me up and daily reflects the woman I wish to become. There would be no ranch without you.

For Katie and Brenda, your love for this orphan is surpassed only by your faithful prayers for me. You are my warriors.

For Sue, thanks for driving, reading, balancing, listening, and…"Up we must go!" Glad there's room on your shoulders for two.

For my Lord, You *are* my Bridge called Hope.

I love you all.

# About the Ranch

Crystal Peaks Youth Ranch is a unique nonprofit organization that rescues abused and neglected horses and pairs them with seeking children. The ranch's program is special in that it almost always pairs one child with one horse, guided by one leader. All this is done free of charge—always.

One of Kim's first riding experiences came on the day of her parents' funeral. In a child's attempt to "ride away" from their murder-suicide, she instead rode straight into the unconditional love of a little horse and a merciful God. As each fully revealed the depth of the other, Kim's life was saved through their combination of healing love.

In 1993, Kim and her husband Troy purchased the only piece of property in Central Oregon that they could afford: a nine-acre, abandoned cinder mine. The land was so completely ruined that no one else wanted it. Together, they began the rehabilitation process by collecting organic waste materials from neighboring ranches.

For two years the Meeders spread moldy hay, used stall shavings, and manure over the rocky floor of the mine to help create a nutritive base that would once again support life. Troy brought home broken and discarded trees, and in 1995, Kim brought home the first two broken and discarded horses. One of them was missing nearly one-third of her normal body weight, while the other had been beaten so badly a vet was needed to suture her beautiful face.

Like shattered shards of stained glass refitted by the hand of God, this broken property…filled with broken trees and broken horses…quietly became the perfect fit to heal the hearts of broken children.

Since its beginning, the ranch has been involved in the rescue of approximately three hundred horses. Today, Crystal Peaks Youth Ranch serves about four thousand visitors a year and is a permanent home for thirty horses. The effectiveness of its impact on kids has been nationally recognized and is being emulated throughout the United States and Canada through Information Clinics held each year at the ranch.

———— ╫ ————

# *Hope is...*

ope is an amazing thing.

It is not only something to aspire to attain, it is also something to aspire to give. Hope becomes a two-edged sword within us. Like a pendulum, it cuts in equal swaths in both directions. One swing cuts a path toward freedom and release, the other toward fulfillment, gratitude, and joy. Either way...

hope gives life.

To the weak, wounded, and crushed in spirit, hope becomes a distant light in the darkness. It is a flicker of radiance that stands in sharp contrast against the blackness of grief, sorrow, and despair. No matter how small its light may appear...there is *no* pain so great that it can stop the light of hope. *No* pain, regardless of how catastrophic and charred it may be...can silence the voice of hope...because...

hope calls us.

Hope's voice calls us through our blackened cavernous places toward its unfathomable brilliance. Initially, hope may appear to balance on the horizon like a diamond, calling with a still, small voice...a voice that knows no silence. When we heed...

hope is our bridge.

Of the giants that live within our soul, one of the most powerful is our ability to *choose*. Throughout our life, choices will rise like bridges, presenting themselves in every known direction. Yet, as bright or black as they may appear...*no one* crosses them for us...we cross alone...propelled by our own will, knowing that...

hope is our choice.

The moment we say yes to hope's voice...and choose with a willing heart to cross its rising bridge beneath us...the diamond once balanced on our horizon bursts forward. Light, truth, and release pour like a sunrise over every crack and crevice of our brokenness. It drenches every shadowed place within us in golden, healing sovereignty.

Like a cleansing fire, hope roils through our dungeons, consuming every chain, bond, and barrier...leaving in its wake...only freedom. This new liberty is not found in filling our blank spaces with answers...but choosing to allow our blank spaces to be filled with peace as truth approaches...because...

hope fills our world.

Every closet, cupboard, and cranny...all lay bare before hope's cleansing brilliance. Its heat within our heart expands, stretching our thoughts, ideas, dreams, and beliefs beyond any boundary previously known.

Hope makes us bigger.

In every honest, balanced, and meaningful way...hope stretches us to a new capacity...a previously unknown capacity to change...

# 1

## *Proof*

Mike looked at me with a completely emotionless expression. I held his gaze. It was not unlike watching ice melt in the sun. The thin ice of his emotional barricade was breaking up beneath him. Clearly, his defenses were beginning to collapse.

Finally, his eyes broke away from mine as all that remained of the "stronghold" beneath him completely shattered.

After taking a deep breath, his gaze wandered to the side. It was clear he was struggling with what he was about to say. Without raising his eyes to look at me, in a voice barely clearing the horizon of a whisper, he said, "I know that you don't love me. You just say that 'cuz you're an adult and it's kinda like your job. But I know you don't *really* love me..." Looking down at nothing, he absently ran his fingers through his dark hair before continuing. "No one loves me...because I can't be loved. I don't...*deserve* to be loved."

I felt like I had been kicked in the gut. No air coming in, no air going out. His pain was so crushing that even from an arm's length away, I could hardly breathe. Suddenly, shoveling rock in the back paddock of the ranch felt heavier than either one of us could bear.

*Girl, get a grip*, I told myself, as I struggled to regain my balance. Mike had risked a great deal to reveal how he felt. He would do that only if he truly wished for me to prove him wrong. *Straighten up, girl! If he wants proof…give it to him!*

All I really knew about Mike was that he came occasionally on Monday with a group from a local juvenile justice facility. Like the other boys in the program, he had earned the right to come to the ranch and volunteer. As with the others, he understood that the ranch was a privilege, one that he treated with respect. In general, he was a quiet kid of approximately sixteen years of age. He appeared to be going through that gawky stage, where his feet and hands were too big for his rapidly growing slender body. His bangs were nearly the length of his nose and he had a subconscious habit of pushing his hair back behind his ears when he needed to focus. Although his brown eyes were murky with caution, he was otherwise polite and engaging.

I could only guess at what might have happened in his life that drove him to this place of ultimate despair. What was said—or worse, done to him—that would make him believe he could not be loved because he didn't deserve it? It was certainly a haunted place that, at the moment, I didn't have time to explore.

Fueled by my lack of wisdom, a quick prayer rose from my heart like a blazing flare: *Lord! I need help…now!* Thankfully, God must be used to my Hail Marys, because what followed in the next hours transformed into something reflecting far greater wisdom than I will ever possess.

Now it was my turn to take a deep breath…and reveal *God's* truth.

"Mike…you're both right…and wrong," I began, while scooping up another shovelful of rocks and tossing them into the bed of the ranch's ATV. "You're right in saying that what comes out of a person's mouth might or might not be true. But you're wrong about your idea that you cannot be loved."

When the bed was running over with cinder, we backed it up to a very precarious ledge halfway up the pit wall, and together dumped the load of rock over the edge to help shore up the road. "You are right in believing that what comes out of a person's mouth can mean anything. But you have to admit that it is what comes out of our *life* that is really true. Mike, our words mean little; it is our actions that prove what is true. Do you agree?" I asked.

His silent response was a slight downturn of his mouth combined with a half-hearted shrug.

"Do you agree, Mike, that it is our actions…not our words… that reveal what is truly inside our hearts?" I prompted again.

"Maybe," he finally conceded.

"Good, because I have something that I want to show you," I said, as I motioned for him to follow me.

Together we entered the main corral and haltered a very large, paint horse named Hanson. I chose this young horse because of his remarkably calm and fun-loving nature. After leading him out to one of the hitching posts, side by side, Mike and I groomed his chestnut and white patched coat. While combing out his mane and tail and cleaning his hooves, I asked Mike many questions, one being that if he could choose, how would he wish for this horse to feel about him.

"He's big! Dude, I wouldn't want him to be mad at me!" he quipped. Then, after a moment, he thoughtfully added, "I would want him to be my friend…"

"Do you think that he wants you to be his friend?" I asked while glancing sideways at him.

A slight but noticeable "tightness" appeared between his

dark eyebrows. I continued to watch as he silently contemplated this concept.

"Okay…are you ready?" I asked, as we led Hanson into the round pen. His expression revealed that he understood that I wasn't really "asking." "Together we are going to round-pen this horse. Since you have never done this before, you have to trust me to 'puppet' you from behind. Okay?"

His look was intent; he was with me.

While standing in the center of the round pen, Mike took in his new surroundings. I watched him turn in a complete circle, as if to confirm that the pen wherein he stood was in fact, round. In every direction rose a solid eight-foot high wall. Answering his question before he asked it, I explained, "The walls are solid to help the horse concentrate on the trainer, and are also a bit safer for his legs as he travels in a circle around us." Mike's gaze was focused on Hanson as he absently nodded in response to this new piece of information.

"You will need to relax and just let me push you from behind. Hey, you should be used to life pushing you around by now!" I laughed as I reached down in the sand to pick up a lunging crop. "We are going to use this crop as an extension of our arm to help communicate with Hanson what we would like him to do. We do not ever use these to whip horses with. Got it?" I asked, as I placed the crop in his right hand and stepped behind him.

Using a round pen to train horses has taught me so much about my own life. Here at the ranch, we use "resistance free" training methods. This means that the horse is free to leave the trainer whenever it wishes. No ropes, leads, or lunge lines are used to connect the horse to the trainer within the circle of the round pen. Because horses are so incredibly sensitive to physical pressure, it is a wonderful way to communicate with them. Although far more complicated, the basic principle boils down to complete simplicity, including which direction you step.

For example, if you step toward a horse, you are pushing them away. If you step away from a horse, you are inviting them into your space. If the horse does not understand you, is stressed, willful, afraid, or playful, it can leave the center of the circle any time it wishes and walk, trot, or canter away in circles around the pen walls.

The down side of leaving the trainer is that the horse must work more. Walking, trotting, or cantering in circles might feel like freedom at first, but once the newness wears off, it just boils down to pure effort that isn't much fun.

Even for a horse, it becomes immediately clear how easy it is to do the right thing and how much more difficult, how much more work it is to do the wrong thing. When the horse is ready to try again, it is free to return to the trainer, because it is here, in the center of the circle, where all the rest, love, peace, joy, and forgiveness are.

Rarely has there been a time in my life that I have worked horses in the round pen when I have not thought how remarkably similar this must be with God's heart and mine. He never stops me from bolting away and running in circles, all the while trying to do things in my own strength. Eventually I become exhausted and realize that *my plan* just isn't working. It is then that I turn back toward the center of the circle and head back to the space that waits for me…right next to God. Because it is here…by His side…where all the rest, love, peace, joy, and forgiveness are.

With one hand gripping his left shoulder and the other around his right wrist, from behind I began to move Mike forward toward Hanson. As I raised Mike's right hand with the crop, right on cue, Hanson began trotting around us. Together, by stepping toward Hanson and raising our crop, we were effectively telling him, "We are gentle but dominant, and would like you to move your feet away from us." As Hanson trotted in a perfect circle around the pen, I asked Mike to look at his eye and ear that was closest to us. "Can you see that his eye is completely fixed on you? Look at the direction of his ear; he is holding it just on you. Right now you have all of his attention. He is waiting for you to tell him what to do next. He's allowing you to be the boss."

Like satin ribbons floating beside him, his long white mane rose and fell with every stride. He was beautiful—there was no denying it. Mike was completely captured by him.

As Hanson continued to move around us, I could feel that Mike's mechanical stiffness was beginning to soften. He was starting to relax not only in my presence but in Hanson's as well. Still puppeting him from behind, I could see vignettes of his profile and that his lips were slightly parted. I leaned forward and spoke very gently near his ear, "Did you know that horses are smarter than people?" Gripping his wrist tighter, I slowly raised the crop within Mike's hand to ask Hanson to continue trotting. I proceeded by carefully stating "A horse *cannot* lie...did you know that?"

Even from my awkward position, I could see that he looked as if he was completely mesmerized by this beautiful creature circling around him. Even blinking seemed to be an interruption for Mike; his gaze on Hanson was completely steady, nearly hypnotic.

Our lesson continued. "Because a horse cannot lie, that means that they can *only* tell the truth." Hanson's circles around us shrank from thirty feet to twenty-five, to twenty, his actions clearly asking if he could join us in the middle. From behind I slowed Mike's walking pace in response, and lowered his crop-laden hand. Still holding his wrist, I extended both of our free hands toward the horse, and together we took a few steps backward, inviting Hanson to come in and join us.

Hanson, who was perhaps twenty feet away, slowed to a stop. He lowered his head slightly, hesitated momentarily then began to slowly walk straight toward Mike. From behind Mike, I slipped the crop out of his hand and silently backed out of the round pen, leaving him in the center with Hanson, alone. They stood face to face, young horse and young boy. Without instruction, Mike instinctively raised his hands and began to rub the giant gelding's forehead. I watched from outside the gate.

It was time.

*God, please show Mike the truth*, I silently prayed as I stepped almost completely from Mike's view behind the round pen wall. "Mike," I called out. "Remember what you said earlier? That you couldn't be loved, that you didn't deserve to be loved? Do you remember saying that?" In this situation, I didn't wish for any subtlety; I wanted this answer for him to be black and white—absolutely concrete.

Even though he didn't really acknowledge my question, it was still clear by his posture that he was listening to me.

"Mike, when you finish petting this horse, I want you to do something for me. I want you to turn around and walk away."

At this strange request, he rotated to look directly at me, his eyebrows crunched together in complete confusion.

"Trust me, Mike. Just do it."

His body language totally changed. He did not want to do this. His formerly relaxed manner began to stiffen against what

I was asking him to do. As if to add emphasis, he pushed his hair behind his ears in a very fast, deliberate motion.

"Come on, buddy, this is part of what I need to show you," I encouraged.

*Lord, everything is riding on this moment. A young man's heart has been stolen. Will you please…in your love…return it to him… full?*

Like a condemned man trudging toward the gallows, Mike walked away from Hanson.

When he could go no farther, he stopped and just stared at the sand that had pushed up against the base of the round pen wall. His body language gave witness to the loveless void that he believed he deserved. In the long shadows of the afternoon, with the world behind him and a solid wall in front of him, he had reached the end of his journey…completely alone.

I wondered if his deserted heart was ringing with the dry echoing of all the abandoned attempts of love that had failed.

His chin was so low that his hair fell forward, concealing most of his face. He stood very still…waiting…perhaps waiting for love to find him. The moment stretched on. Slowly, it began to feel too long, dusty, and parched with anticipation.

Piece by piece, all the world seemed to go completely silent…as if holding its breath in a unified hope that a young man's belief in a lie…would be broken.

Suddenly, Mike jumped as if he had been electrocuted! Two huge, damp nostrils had momentarily pressed against the back of his neck. Hanson's choice had been made…and he chose love…through the companionship of a broken young man.

Mike let a startled swear word fly as he jerked around to find Hanson looming directly behind him. With one hand on his heart, he exhaled in relief, "Dude! You can't sneak up on me like that!" As Mike regained his composure, he began to pet the giant who had chosen to follow him.

With a big sigh, I, too, realized that my hand was covering my heart.

*Lord, let your truth fall like a hammer. Break the lies that bind...let Your light pour into the darkness...so blind eyes can see*, I prayed before I continued.

"Since you said that you don't really believe that I love you, maybe you will believe someone else." I paused to let this concept settle in his heart. "As far as your idea of not being able to be loved, I think that Hanson has something to say to you about that." I took a deep breath. "Mike, this horse is completely free to go anywhere he wants to, and since you *believe* that you 'don't deserve to be loved,' I want you to walk away from him...again."

As before, Mike walked with arduous steps nearly as far away as he could...*nearly*. Without hesitation, Hanson turned and walked closely behind him. "Mike, turn around and look," I said softly. He knew that the horse was following him, and without a word, turned and reached up, running his hand under the horse's mane.

I clarified the scene: "He cannot tell you how he feels with words...so he is telling you with his actions. Again, Mike, I don't want you to have any doubt...so walk away again," I quietly added.

This time, he left his hand resting on the top of the gelding's neck and they walked away together.

"He is a horse...he cannot lie...he can *only* tell you the truth, Mike...and he is telling you something right now. He is clearly saying without a word that you are wrong; not only *can* you be loved...he is *choosing* to love you...because you *are* worth it."

I wondered, when Mike stopped, if he had not purposefully turned his back toward me. With his face turned away, he
stood leaning heavily against Hanson's neck.

*Let your hammer fall, Lord...*

"Mike...keep walking...I want you to keep walking away
for as long as it takes for you to really *believe* what is true...
because honestly, what is true...your *proof*...is following you.
With every step he is *proving* you wrong...with every step he is
asking to be your friend...to be in your herd...to be your family. Keep walking until you are ready to let go of your belief that
you cannot be loved. Then you can stop...and embrace what
you now *know* is true."

Nearly before I had finished speaking, Mike had stopped
and turned into Hanson's mane. Again, his back was toward me.
I watched as he slipped one arm over the top of the gelding's
neck and one arm under, encircling him in a silent embrace.

He had come home…to the middle…where all the rest, love, peace, joy, and forgiveness are.

Without a sound, Mike's shoulders began to shudder. Like Jericho, the once impenetrable walls of his prison began to crumble under the unfathomable weight of truth, love, freedom. Tears of release began to fall.

There, within the privacy of the round pen, the "hammer" fell…pounding into powder the stronghold of deception that had formerly enslaved a boy. The river of truth poured in, enveloping a young man's heart in a deluge of relief. The flood came and returned that same heart…filled to overflowing… proving that the power of God's love knows no bounds.

Hanson, without a single word, spoke truth into the life and heart of a young man. What was once broken and empty began to again bask in the warmth of unconditional love. It was a love without price or terms, a love without strings or conditions…arriving in peaceful silence from the *Author* of love.

Perhaps to all others the scene looked much like a young man holding a young horse…yet, from my perspective it was clear…a young hostage was being set free.

# 2

## Side by Side

I t was early January. Lying quietly—and frozen under a silent layer of white—the ranch basked in weak rays of winter sunshine.

The call for help came into our ranch office just after lunch. As usual, Faith, the receptionist, answered the phone. Only moments later she shared with me how she had taken notes at a frantic pace in an effort to keep up with the impassioned woman on the other end of the line. Apparently the woman was a neighbor of some folks who owned horses on a piece of property that connected with their own. It sounded like they even shared the same driveway. The focus of the conversation centered on how she had been pleading with local organizations for approximately fourteen months to please come and intervene for the starving horses next door. According to her, one of them had just died. Her simple request remained the same: "Can you please come and help?"

Nearly everyone who was on the ranch responded by loading up into the truck while I ran to the house to get my camera. When I returned, Faith, Marie, and Karmen were in the cab waiting for me.

While driving to the location, I realized that none of these young women had ever been on a rescue team before. As we navigated the snowy roads, I briefed the girls as to what their "job" would be once we reached the scene. It was vitally important that we document everything, food source, water source, fencing, injuries, body condition. "See...*all* of the scene," I encouraged.

The scene was only a few miles away, and we arrived much more quickly than we expected. The four remaining horses were in front of the ramshackle house and they were, indeed, in very bad condition. There was no evidence of a carcass. Perhaps the horse that had perished had done so earlier in the week.

Being unannounced and uninvited, I took advantage of what appeared to be no one at home and used a ridiculous amount of time just turning the truck around in their driveway. "Look...see everything, girls...this might be our only chance for a while," I instructed, while bringing the truck around.

We noticed that it had lightly snowed the night before, giving our detective work a timeline.

I could see two bales of hay pushed under a dilapidated tractor trailer. One bale was opened and, as of this morning, a single, large flake of hay had been tossed into the corral. I assumed this was all that they had been fed for the day. One four-inch-thick square of hay to feed four horses! That amount was not even sufficient for *one* horse in warm weather.

Having already assumed that no one was home, we were all a bit surprised when a woman came walking toward the truck while pulling on a coat. "What do we do?! We're caught on their property!" Marie burst out.

"We're okay...all is well...everyone calm down and treat her with great respect and kindness...understood?" I reassured in a quiet voice. Solemn nods were my reward as I turned my attention back to the woman who was approaching my door.

After powering my window down, I shut the truck engine off so we could speak. "Hello, I hope that I am not intruding on your day…I couldn't help but notice that you have some wonderful horses here…" The woman's puzzled expression relaxed as I commented on how beautiful her two black and white pinto mares were. I noticed she also owned a very thin older mare and what looked like an emaciated weanling black filly.

"I can be such a sap when it comes to pretty horses…obviously, I cannot drive by them," I said, while still trying to put our host at ease.

Perhaps realizing that we came in peace, the woman softened into a gracious host and invited all of us to leave the truck and enter the corral to pet her "babies." I was very aware that while I engaged the woman, my staff was running their hands over each of the horses and mentally recording every detail.

While in the starving horses' corral, I noticed that a light breeze had scattered the meager serving of hay across the pen. A small handful had blown within the tiny black filly's reach. She silently moved toward the dozen or more straws of hay to consume them as quickly as possible. She ate as if her life depended on it, and by the looks of her skeletal form…it most certainly did.

The woman was more than happy to share with me how she had acquired her horses and what her future plans were with each one of them. As she continued to rattle off personal accounts of training adventures, I inconspicuously moved to the filly's shoulder and placed my open hand on her withers. This is usually one of the safest and most non-threatening places to touch an unfamiliar horse. For young horses, it is also reminiscent of the favored place for a mother to lovingly groom her foal. Sadly, for this young horse, it was obvious that she was not accustomed to human touch.

Once the filly understood that it was a strange woman who was touching her, she instantly swung her head in an attempt to bite me. She missed. It was clear that even in her weakened state, she was going to fight me for those few stems of hay that had blown her way. With her expression she seemed to warn me, "I will die if I don't eat this…it's all I have."

*Poor baby girl* I thought to myself, as I gently and cautiously stroked her neck, shoulder, and back.

With more effort than it should have taken, she drove her abnormally sharp hip bone toward me in a weak but aggressive move that clearly communicated that she would kick me if she could. I kept my hand firmly on her repulsively bony hip and stood fast. With this little girl, had I stepped back I would have placed myself in a position where she truly could have kicked me. Also, my moving away from her threat would have not only rewarded her bad behavior, in horse language it would have told her that she was undoubtedly the boss.

The owner didn't seem to notice any of this and continued to share with me one horse story after another. Finally, during an appropriate break in our conversation, I asked her plainly, "Would you ever consider selling any of your horses?" Her eyes moved very slowly upward in a near forty-five-degree angle. She blinked a few times and then abruptly returned her gaze to me. "Maybe," she finally answered.

After extremely gentle negotiations, we were able to convince the owner to sell us the very worst of the four starving equines—the black filly. Like a carrot dangling from a fishing pole, the promise of hay and cash was enough for her to finally oblige our request.

The girls were wonderful; each thoughtfully shook the woman's hand and thanked her for her time and generosity in sharing her "family" with us. After climbing back into the truck, I started the engine and we all waved good-bye, promising to return as soon as possible to pick up the filly.

Once we were down the driveway, everyone nearly exploded in a released rush of information. Each of the girls did an excellent job in gathering and reporting the details that they noticed. Once the flourish of words died down, Karmen, who was quiet by nature, began to speak. The intense contrast between her clear blue eyes and dark hair always seemed to give her words a greater impact, a weightiness beyond their casual meaning. She said very quietly, almost to herself, "We're getting the right one…it's the little filly that is suffering the most."

I reminded the girls that we needed to hurry because a greater time lapse offers owners a greater time frame to change their minds about releasing their horses. Although it is not a common occurrence, it has happened in the past.

During our return trip back to the ranch, we organized the completion of the rescue. Every member of the team was given a specific job to help facilitate the quick and safe release of this devastated little horse. Once at the ranch, I would hitch up the trailer and Karmen would help me load up as much hay as it would hold. Marie was responsible to find as much cash in the office as she could, while Faith made the appropriate calls to clear an opening in our time frame.

After all these tasks had been completed, our small team reunited at the cab of the truck, kicked the snow off our boots, and slid inside. While traveling back to recover the filly, we choreographed all our following actions.

Marie is remarkably funny and likable—and volunteered to gather the necessary paperwork. She would encourage the owner indoors to write up a usable bill of sale. While the two were inside, Karmen, Faith, and I would quickly unload the hay. Because of the potential danger, I would halter the filly and lead her out of the corral. Once out of the corral, Karmen and Faith would assist me in helping to load the young horse into the trailer.

As we drove down the drive toward the hungry horses, I noticed something interesting. Karmen saw it too. She turned back to look at me, perhaps wondering if I was thinking the same thing. I glanced at the horses and back at her...and smiled. In her quiet way, she smiled back and stated what we were both looking at: "The filly is waiting at the gate."

Only two hours after the initial call for help, in what was surely a horse-recovery speed record, we were pulling up the driveway with the first rescued horse of the year.

Even though she was documented to be nearly two years of age, her actual size was that of a six-month-old baby. As a young quarter horse filly, she should have weighed twice her desperate 440 pounds. Her flesh hung from her spine like a sagging canvas over a tent pole. On this diminutive waif, the normally graceful arc that connects a horse's head to its neck looked more like an old boot hanging on a broomstick. Her hooves were so small they didn't even come close to filling the palm of my hand.

Her dull coat was nearly three inches long with large bald patches on either side of her neck. Her oozing and crusted skin was completely destroyed by one of the worst lice infestations I had ever seen. The poor little babe was literally being eaten alive by parasites.

Adding to her woes was the fact that her previous water source was a large galvanized tank with a dilapidated hose frozen tightly into an eight-inch-thick solid block. The ice was so old that it had substantially pulled away from the edges of the tank. As near as we could estimate by the length of the last deep cold spell, she had not had a drink of water for approximately eleven to thirteen days.

It is not possible for a horse to live that long without water, but mercifully, two weeks before, her saving grace fell in the form of snow. The frozen white surface in her former corral had the pocked appearance of a giant golf ball. Literally thousands of fist-sized holes could be seen where all four of the horses had tried to stem their thirst by eating mouthfuls of snow.

Thankfully, all went like clockwork. While Marie went into the house with the filly's owner to get a bill of sale, the girls and I worked together like wheeled cogs in getting the hay out of the trailer...and getting the filly in. I am uncertain if it was the tantalizing hay all over the trailer floor, or if this filly somehow comprehended that getting into this box was going to change her life forever. Either way, she was astoundingly eager to hop up into the waiting trailer. I noticed that once we secured the door behind the filly, Karmen became particularly anxious to leave. While looking in the direction of the house where Marie and the owner were apparently wrapping things up, she muttered, "What's taking so long? Let's get outta here."

In her weakened condition, the simple act of being moved the few miles back to our ranch, height and weight taped, photographed, and vaccinated taxed the black filly to complete fatigue. Once all was finished, Karmen slowly led her into the ranch quarantine paddock. After a very long drink of water and a few bites of hay, our tiny new charge collapsed in utter exhaustion.

Because the weather was bitter, her new home, which was approximately twenty by forty yards, came complete with a heated water tank and a three-sided wind shelter full of clean, dry shavings. Perhaps because she had never known the use of a shelter before, she didn't choose its warm comforts, but instead crumpled into the windblown snow. Her condition was so severe at this point that I wondered if she might die. Her tattered black form lay in sharp contrast against the pure white snow upon which she chose to rest.

Yet, removed from her familiar hell, in this strange new world, she was alone.

Perhaps, of the four women on the rescue team, Karmen understood the black filly the most. At fifteen years of age, she was the youngest. Karmen had been coming to the ranch off and on for several years with her severely disabled sister. Now, she was coming solely for herself. With very focused intent, she sought help in traversing the lonely bridge away from her chosen life of self injury. I will always remember the day that she asked for my help.

I have seen it before, it's called cutting. Insidious and permanent, it is the dangerous, newly revealed scourge moving through the underbelly of our country. Like an invisible plague, its only purpose is to destroy those it haunts. If attempted suicide were a sibling, cutting would be its desperate little brother, both silently screaming for help. Cutting is a symbolic ritual of releasing pain, guilt, anger, shame, or sorrow through slashing one's own skin with a sharp blade and literally bleeding it out. It is the external equivalent of an internal agony.

The first time Karmen showed me her scars, it would have been easy to assume that she had a serious encounter with a barbed wire fence…and lost. Her forearms and lower legs bore the marks of her torment. Some marks were old and faded into a normal flesh tone. Others were purple or pink—or worse, a recent, shiny bright red. She told me how, collectively, they all mocked her, daring her to go deeper each time, taunting her for being a coward and not just "doing it"…not just ending her life. She, as do all cutters, understood what the approaching ultimate conclusion of this behavior would be. Karmen knew that she needed help…soon.

Cutting would destroy her; she knew that. Yet removed from her familiar hell, in this strange new world, she, too, felt very much alone.

Quietly standing outside the quarantine paddock, Karmen's freezing breath rose around her as she watched the solitary young horse lying on her sternum, motionless in the snow. Karmen silently rested her chin on her arms, which were folded over the top of the gate. She was completely motionless. Loneliness is a dark, cold prison. Those who have escaped its abandoned walls know that the only key is not found within…but without. Only by honestly giving of one's self in true friendship can true friendship honestly be received.

After an achingly long, cold moment, Karmen straightened to her full height and with the soothing hush of the quiet breeze that moved around her, silently made her way to the collapsed filly's side. Sacrificing her own safety and comfort, a broken young woman lay down in the snow, side by side with a broken young horse.

The utterly spent filly, sensing and taking comfort in the girl's presence, relaxed even further. Her large brown eyes began to slowly blink and flag downward. Her neck, as if pulled by an unseen force, gradually curved downward toward the ground. The filly, in a final expression of exhaustion, finally rolled over, inch by inch, until she was lying completely flat on her side. In moments, the young horse was overwhelmed by sleep.

As the filly rolled toward her, Karmen stealthily matched her movements until her chest was against the prone horse's back. Karmen, now in full contact with the filly, watched in complete wonder as her new friend slipped deeper into her blissful escape. Fascination overtook her as she observed the tiny horse begin to jerk, blink, and twitch. There, with snow as her bed, the worn-out equine began to dream.

A new realization rose within Karmen's heart. Despite all the trauma and heartache this devastated little horse had been through, even through all her lack and failure…she still had dreams.

Karmen shared with me later that it was at this time, this exact moment, that she began to feel the battlefield within her heart quietly subside. It was during this incredibly special "mirroring" that she started to reconcile the fact that if this young, broken horse was still fighting for her dreams…perhaps it was time for the young, broken girl…to do the same.

So there, with snow as her bed, the worn out girl extended the arm that had been supporting her head, laid down flat, closed her eyes…and began to dream.

Karmen relayed to me that it was as if she could feel the clenched fists inside her heart begin to slowly open…into hands that reached out to the One who was calling her toward safety, freedom, release, and love. In that cold and quiet time that followed, Karmen understood that this was the time to *choose* to let go of her pain, anger, frustration, and sorrow.

She said that she felt like she was waging a war within her chest. All her negative emotions came fighting forward, battling for nothing less than her imminent destruction. Yet still lying there next to that little filly, she felt empowered. Strengthened by the determination of a tiny black horse and a merciful God, it was then that she realized her life was worth fighting for… and fight she did.

Her eyes shone with fire as she shared how she silently called her emotional demons to come forth, one by one, and faced her new resolution of strength given by the Lord. Every emotion that fought for destructive control of her life, she called forward and symbolically destroyed them with the very blade that they had been using to destroy her. When she was finished, she said that it seemed like remnants of sorrow, pain, bitterness, loneliness, anger, and grief surrounded her on the snow like broken leaves. Barring that she would choose to pick them up and reconstruct them, each one lay mortally broken around her.

A late afternoon breeze moved through the pines overhead. Their tranquil music was the only voice that drifted over the white, frozen ranch. Cradled together by the unmistakable lullaby of God whispering down through the trees, two weary hearts rested against each other. It was a new start for both.

Below the boughs, resting together in a newly forged sense of freedom and peace, side by side in the snow, lay a young dreaming horse and a young dreaming girl.

Not long after, a few of the rescue team came into the bunkhouse for lunch and warmed themselves by the wood-stove. Ideas of what might be an appropriate name for the new black filly circulated. "Solstice" quickly rose to the top of the list. Her rescue came only two weeks after the winter solstice. It seemed only fitting. She had survived the darkest days of her life. From this day forward, each day would be a little brighter than the last.

While the crew was finishing up lunch, Karmen arrived. I asked her what she thought of that idea. She remained silent and thoughtful for long moments. Perhaps the image of brighter days was slowly finding its way into her heart as well. Or maybe she, too, was considering a symbolic name change.

Finally, in cool, quiet, typical Karmen style, with a half smile and a nearly imperceptible nod, she simply stated, "It's good."

---

*Young Wisdom*

Joshua, age 9:
"There are only two kinds of people in this world...
those who pick their nose...and *liars*."

# 3

## Bright Spot

As faithful as a sunrise, little Lucas ran straight toward me, stopping only when he crashed into my thigh with a little-boy hug. He looked up at me momentarily, then quickly tucked his chin straight down into his chest. Clearly, this was his wordless invitation, summoning me to continue my "tradition."

Not wanting to disappoint, I cupped his blond head between my hands. With great drama and ceremony, I hummed all the way until my lips touched the top of his head in a great big kiss. *Mmmwah!* I let him go as if I had been shocked by the impact. He looked back up at me with immeasurable delight…laughed once, then ran away.

It is no secret that I love kids. Most of my days gleam with the combined brilliance that these little stars carry within their hearts. Some shine with the blinding glare of a supernova, while others blink with the little twinkle of a matchstick. Despite their diversity, they are all little bright lights that continually flood my life with their unique brand of sunshine.

Most who know me understand that I love to hug and kiss. Being raised by my grandmother, I learned from the master herself. A sincere hug or a well-placed kiss can communicate a book of words in a single moment. And for many, I often wonder if they have been held close by anyone since they saw me last.

As for kissing, my absolute favorite place is the top of the head. I am tall and kids are short, and it just makes sense that this is the perfect non-threatening place for me to kiss them. Many kids who frequent the ranch are yet unable to verbally ask for a kiss, but they wish for one nonetheless. These are my precious little ones who run up to me and either tuck under my arm and wait, or bow slightly forward, silently offering me their best kissing pose. For me, no matter how it transpires throughout the day, kissing kids is always a bright spot.

———— ｜｜ ————

Another beautiful afternoon was winding down toward conclusion. It had been a long and somewhat difficult day filled with much physical labor and many emotional challenges. I was scheduled to meet two women. One, who I already knew well, was bringing a friend who was going through a tough season. Her intention was for me to give encouragement and support to her struggling friend.

I didn't realize until after my guests arrived how completely exhausted I felt. After simple introductions, I led my two visitors away from the happy mayhem that surrounded the center of the ranch toward one of the picnic tables that had been pulled under the shade of a nearby locust tree. I was hoping this location might offer us a slightly more quiet and private place for the new guest to share her feelings.

I smiled to myself as the three of us approached the wooden table. It had recently been painted a lovely forest green by volunteers. What made me smile was a cartoon that had been painted on top. It was of a goofy bi-plane pulling a banner that stretched most of the length of the tabletop and read, "Crystal Peaks Youth Ranch...You'll love it here!"

Sensing the heaviness in my new guest, I had already decided to sit the closest to her. Once we sat down together, I immediately recognized my mistake. Those closest to me understand that the more exhausted I am, the more fractured my thought processes, and the more difficulty I have staying focused. My mistake was guiding my guests to the table and allowing them to sit with their backs to the ranch...which meant I would be facing all the happy tangle of activities behind them. This is the vantage point I normally choose, but in my weary state I knew I was about to struggle greatly to hear and comprehend what these woman came to share with me. I understand that it takes great courage to share painful family issues with a stranger, and I did not wish for any details of our conversation to be lost.

I stepped over the bench and straddled it like a horse so I could fully engage face-to-face the woman who was having a difficult time and needed the most encouragement.

The area behind her was flowing with happy pursuits. Every available leader was paired with a child, and all were whirling within various stages of ranch activity.

Although we sat to the side of the main yard on the grass, my view encompassed the entire mid-section of the ranch. To my right was the main herd corral, tacking area, and activities barn. Straight ahead was the main yard, and just beyond was the grassy hill where the kids bathe the horses, engage in squealing water fights, and have summersault races. To my left was the bunkhouse, riding arena, round pen, and another bathing lawn that was currently filled with wet kids and horses.

Many more "mini groups" of volunteers were busy administering their unique gifts to this simple little place. Adding to the grinning mayhem was a dear friend who serenaded all on her violin with her cheerful fiddling. Funny how music changes everything. Suddenly, for some, pulling weeds became a moment to "swing yer pardner"...even if your partner was a weed! It was so fun for my guests and me to watch for a moment as the entire ranch seemed to rise to the music that played across it.

Slowly, the women's conversation moved toward family issues—the true reason for this visit. My meandering attention yanked back to the woman in front of me. Her tone was becoming more serious, and I could see her eyes beginning to shine with gathering tears.

*Concentrate, Kim!* I commanded myself. *This woman is being courageous enough to give her heart...now you need to be focused enough to give her your attention!*

I peered intently into the woman's face as she continued speaking. Her words were flowing out of her mouth, but not into my ears. My gaze strained to stay within the outline of her jaw, until it broke loose again. *Wow, what a wonderful horse and child combination that is!* I thought, as I glanced over toward the hitching post...

Kim! Focus!

Within my fatigue-hammered heart, I was dumbfounded and a little saddened at how little of what this woman was saying was actually entering my head. I felt like a brainless test dummy for some weird hypnosis experiment. *Just stare at the lips…keep your eyes on the lips…*

Suddenly, Lucas ran up behind the woman I was straining to focus on. He was not even three feet behind her when he stepped up onto a railroad tie that encircled a flower bed and yanked down his pants! Completely oblivious to us, with the innocence and abandonment of a three-year-old, he began to "water the flowers"! This child was maybe seven feet away from me! I could feel my eyes ping-pong back and forth between the crying woman and the peeing boy!

Not wishing to minimize the importance of the account being shared, I struggled even more to maintain my focus. Now my internal free-for-all began to pressurize as I fought hard not to smile or burst out laughing in the face of a distraught woman! I could sense that my face was turning bright red. With great difficulty, I was managing the task…until the little imp began *sky writing!*

Thankfully, all good things must come to an end. I was exactly one moment away from discovering if a human being can actually blow her own head off with explosive laughter… when my little "high flyer" finished his mission, returned everything to its proper place, and pulled his pants back up.

My relief spread like a hound on a porch. I could feel the muscles in my jaw begin to relax and the natural shape of my mouth returning. Obviously, seeing my ridiculous facial contortions, the sweet-but-distressed woman in front of me must have thought I was either the biggest drama queen on earth or the most over-emotional sap she had ever seen!

All was going well again—until my little blond friend, who was still standing within arm's reach of my guests, realized that his hand was "wet." I stealthily observed him study his wet hand. He just didn't seem to know what to do. His little brain churned with the realization that to wipe pee on your own clothes would be yucky.

So, according to his three-year-old sense of logic, he did the next best thing. He wiped dry his pee-soaked hand…on his head. The *top* of his head…on the exact spot that I had just kissed!

# 4

## Littlest Bear

Once again, fall was descending on the high desert. Each frosty night gave way to a new dawn full of more color than the last. The trees on the ranch seemed to join in an unwritten melody, all singing together, through their dramatic transformation, of the sheer glory of life. Each year I can't help but imagine that this is how nature gives one last glorious "hoorah!" before the deep rest of winter's white falls.

After walking up the hill toward our home, I kicked the edge of the deck to clean off my boots before going inside. Like taking a deep breath, I took one last, long look at the view. I was deeply struck by how the simplicity of man-made things was absolutely no match for the magnificent autumn wonder that clothed the ranch below. Anyone who knows me understands how much more my heart desires to stay in God's masterpiece of creation...than to go into my office. But, we do what we must to keep going forward.

Following my evening routine of taking off my hat and putting my sunglasses inside, it was time to finally sit. While leaning back in my office chair, I put my boots on the edge of my desk and thumbed through my daily messages. Immediately, a note confirming that Virginia had called earlier caught my attention. Virginia and her twin sister, Vicki, are close friends who work together on an enormous horse ranch just ten miles west of ours. Knowing my friend, she usually calls when she has a fun, horse-related message. I returned her call first.

She began by explaining that she and her sister had just returned home from a "buyers" trip to a Canadian PMU farm. Her rapid-fire recount of the trip quite suddenly came to an abrupt pause. "Please know that what I am about to share with you in no way obligates you or your ranch in any way. In our purchase, we acquired a very special little horse that I would love for you to come and see…"

I whipped my hat back on my head before it was cold. I quickly rationalized, "Dinner is overrated and any excuse is good enough for me to go and look at horses." Laughing to myself, I shoved a power bar into my pocket and headed back out the front door.

While driving the distance between our two ranches, I tried to piece together all of the fragments of information that Virginia had just given me. I wasn't sure what I was about to see when I arrived at her place. They had just brought down one hundred weanlings, who were now in a very large corral recuperating from their 1,200-mile journey.

In addition to being identical twins, Virginia and Vickie are well known in Central Oregon for many things. Together with their employer, they purchased the freedom of several hundred industry horses and brought them home to begin a new life in Oregon.

Aside from their excellent work ethic and easy humor, they, more than all others combined, have brought PMU awareness and action to our beautiful state.

PMU is an acronym for Pregnant Mare Urine, which is

the source of hormones used to create the enormously popular hormone replacement therapy drug called Premarine. It's also used in many over-the-counter "anti-aging" cosmetics. Harvesting mare urine for these products has been going on for the last sixty years. This is done by placing mares in a specialized "collection" stall. This space, which becomes their home for six months or more, is not wide enough for them to turn around in or lay down flat. Once they deliver their foal, the mares are immediately rebred, because it is only when they are pregnant that they produce the highly sought-after hormones. The resulting foals, especially the colts, are of little value to these farms, and are routinely sent to feedlots where most are sold for slaughter.

Seeing the great need to intervene for these imperiled foals, Virginia and Vicki began their mission. By purchasing quantities of weanling colts and fillies, they initially hoped to train them up for numerous "dude strings" throughout the area. As these young horses entered the community and started proving themselves, their popularity began to soar.

As most who have ever owned animals understand, it is relatively easy to find homes for young, cute, pliable individuals. Sadly, the aged, broken, and fearful ones do not have this ease afforded to them.

When studies revealed that cancer could be linked to Hormone Replacement Therapy treatment, drug sales dropped dramatically and suddenly 30,000 PMU mares were out of work. At their age, and being large, heavy horses with virtually no training or socialization, nearly all were in grave peril of being slaughtered.

When the devastating news of the PMU mares' jeopardy reached Virginia and Vicki, they did more than just feel bad for them. Instead of only "feeling," they *acted*.

In what could perhaps be an Oregon-to-Alberta-to-Oregon turnaround speed record, they purchased as many mares as their convoy could move. Their final tally was 240 pregnant mares—all of whom now have a safe home and will never be in danger of slaughter again. However, any accolade that might be given to either of the dynamic twins would just be matter-of-factly shrugged off. While punctuated with an expression of satisfaction, they would merely view it as all in another day's work.

Even though PMU farms have been in existence since 1942, it has only been in the last decade that urine harvesting practices have been more readily revealed. The horses involved in this industry are primarily heavy draft and draft crosses. This is to ensure greater volumes of urine per horse. A fifteen-hundred-pound mare will produce more than a nine hundred-pound mare.

The horses are fitted with one of two methods of collection. Either they are internally cauterized or they are fitted with an external device. The hose that exits their body empties into a plastic container outside the horse's stall.

To create a greater concentration of estrogen in the urine, the horses are given only a limited amount of water. This combined with trying to grow a foal with little or no exercise often results in severe infections within the mare's liver and kidneys. Although most horses' normal life span is around thirty years of age, it is not uncommon for PMU mares to not survive past the second trimester of life because of their abnormal stress load.

Until recently, most of the surviving colt population was sold to the slaughter market, while the fillies would be kept to replace their rapidly depleting mothers. All this equine woe continues today in support of an antiquated drug that has already been replicated synthetically in a much purer form. It has been estimated that since its inception, more than one million horses have perished within this industry.

Currently, many PMU farms will host an annual autumn foal sale. Some do this solely to boost their bottom line and some because they honestly wish a better life for the livestock that supports them. Either way, things are slowly beginning to change for the horses born into this archaic industry.

One of the foundations for this change is the widespread recognition that these draft-crossed babies grow up into incredibly versatile horses. As they filter into the working horse world, they are turning heads as remarkable trail, mountain, pack, and all-around family horses. Because of their impressive size, bone structure, and movement, they are commanding respect in nearly every show venue as well.

My attention snapped back to Virginia, who was waiting for me when I pulled into her driveway only moments later. In unison, we entered the corral where all of her new arrivals were munching on hay.

As we walked amongst them, they parted before us like a dodging school of very large fish. While we strolled together, we briefly discussed the current status of the remaining PMU farms. Within this conversation, my friend laughed at her own joke: "I mean really…what woman would knowingly want to rub horse pee all over her face or dose it down with a glass of water?"

Virginia went on to fill in the details of her earlier account. "The ranch where we buy these youngsters is 1,200 miles away, deep within the province of Alberta in Canada. It is located not far from the foot of the Canadian Rockies…beautiful, but wild. During our few days at the PMU farm, they shot five bears that had become so brazen that they were coming in and killing the horses. Because of the horses' confinement, they had become easy targets for the marauding bears. Many of the foals did not survive.

"While we were in Canada, our hosts drove approximately three hundred pairs of mares and foals into the squeeze chutes to be sorted apart from each other. As they came through the chutes, Vicki and I had about thirty seconds per foal to determine if we wanted to buy them. Instantly they were released into another large holding pen where they were permanently separated from their mother."

I could hear Virginia's voice change subtly as she shifted her thoughts toward the reason why I was there. "The mothers and babies always come through together, usually with the mother in front of the foal. One pair came through and a wrangler noticed that the foal had sustained a bear attack. The colt's whole hind end was involved, with most of the extensive damage done on his left rump and hamstring. They were going to 'cull' him out, which usually means an unfortunate end…but I just couldn't let that happen.

"When I saw him, I was surprised at how small he was. He couldn't have been more than a few months old. He still needed to be at his mother's side. I just felt like he was pleading for my help. He could survive these wounds if he was given a chance. That's all he needed…just a chance."

"That's when I thought of you…and felt that if he could survive the two-day trip home, smashed in with dozens of others who were twice his size, he was meant to be yours." As she looked at me, I could see that her heart had been greatly moved by this tiny colt.

"At every sale there is a veterinarian present to inspect each animal that will cross the border into the U.S. They are instructed to pull all horses that exhibit any lumps, bumps, obvious swelling, or open wounds. We had three foals pulled from our herd because of random swellings. I had hardly finished telling the hosts that I would gladly pay to have this pitiful little colt vetted until he was cleared for travel, when suddenly the attending vet just waved him on through as 'fit to continue.'

"We loaded up the 'kids' and drove six hours to the U.S. line, and then had to unload everyone for their final border inspection. For the second time in a day, an inspector looked right at him and gave the order to load him back into the trailer!

"I never thought that I would be happy to have a truckload of muddy babies...but I realize now that I sure am grateful for all the muck on the littlest one! Who knew that a little well-placed mud on a wound could open palace doors?"

Bathed in the beautiful light of early evening, Virginia and I continued our search through the herd for this special little babe who had already survived so much. The enclosure for the young horses was very large and supplied with a half dozen or more giant bales of hay for the youngsters to free-choice graze from. Even in their exhaustion, the horses were still wary of human approach. The entire corral moved like a lazy river of shifting, eating, and napping infants. "You won't believe it when you see him...he is such a cutie patutie!"

I laughed out loud at her trademark nickname of adoration.

"Look for the smallest baby in the herd; he is a beautiful buckskin. Did I mention that he has a wide blaze and three high white socks?"

I glanced at Virginia. She amazed me. Her brain was a virtual horse-sorting computer. In all her years of dealing with horses, *thousands of horses*, she never forgot a single detail, not a snipe, a blaze, a sock, or a stripe. She remembered them all, each for their very best attributes, each with much affection.

"There he is!" she said, and pointed to a small herd of about a dozen youngsters who were moving away from us.

I looked but saw no buckskin among them. I looked back at Virginia and verified the direction she was pointing, but still did not see him. When we turned directly toward the small group, they parted like a flock of birds. Virginia was right; hidden amongst the bigger, stronger weanlings was a tiny golden baby.

My enthusiasm to finally see him was momentarily interrupted when his hind end came fully into my view. As he turned and began moving directly away from me, I could clearly see the injuries on both sides of his rump. Although the gashes on his right rump were partially hidden by mud and hair, the left rump injury was over a foot long vertically, with a fist-sized chunk of flesh that was bitten right out of the middle. It was horrifyingly unmistakable. How could anyone with two eyes not see this?

*Dear Lord…how has this infant survived?* I thought, as I noticed a dry trail of bloody serum nearly the width of my arm crusted down the remaining length of his leg.

I could hardly speak. He *was* small! His tiny stature was supported on stilt-like legs with gigantic knees and even bigger feet. He moved with the same huge-footed "flippity-floppity" gait of a large-breed puppy — the same kind of puppy that makes everyone look at its feet and say, "Holy Cow! This one's going to be a *monster*!" The colt's legs were heavily feathered with long, silky hair, indicating that he was a draft.

Before I could comment, he turned his head slightly back to look at me. With that distinctively crested profile, there was no doubt he was not only a draft breed…he was a Clydesdale!

I felt a bit like an adoptive parent who was seeing her child for the first time. All his unique shortcomings, through the eyes of a "mother," became invisible. Beneath my own breath, I finally said, "There he is…my little boy."

I was acutely aware that Virginia was watching my reaction. The sheer "wattage" from her smile could not be measured. Perhaps when she first saw him, her response had been similar to mine. After several moments, my voice returned. "He's a buckskin Clyde? How can that be?" I asked after menally tallying that Clydesdales only come in variations of black, bay, and roan.

"You're right" she confirmed. "Clydesdales cannot make this color pattern. I have met his sire, who is a stunning seventeen-hand red roan Clyde. This baby's color must have somehow come through his mother, who I believe was a draft quarter horse cross."

I couldn't take my eyes off him. He moved in such a floundering way. Each leg seemed to be traveling in a different direction than the others. He was young…really young. I couldn't help but wonder how much of his awkward movement was due to his age…or his injuries. Virginia was right about this one; truly, all he needed was a chance.

———+|+———

Once the baby Clyde was settled in his new home on the ranch, we named him "Little Bear" in honor of his remarkable past. I realized that his name would soon become a joke, because his feet clearly indicated that he wasn't going to be little for very long!

Instinct had taught this youngster that if he was to survive, he needed to protect his injuries. Even though he quickly accepted me, my staff, and the ranch kids, he did not want anyone to touch him from his shoulders back. This posed an obvious problem if we were going to attempt to vet this little man.

As with much in life, consistency is the key. Daily, I would enter his corral and offer him a pan of grain. While he ate, I would gently brush his face, neck and shoulders. If I was alone, having a voice that only a horse could appreciate, I would sing songs for him. Gradually, I would allow the brush to travel a little farther down his body with each soothing stroke. With every little "victory" I would reward him with a massage on the top of his withers.

After a few weeks, our goal was achieved and he would allow gentle touching around his injury. The day soon came when I entered his corral armed with a bucket of warm water, clean rags, sharp scissors, and some ointment, it was time to clean his wounds. Julie, one of the ranch staff, steadied his front end with one hand and brushed him with the other. Even though he was a bit anxious at times, he was a brave little soul and allowed me full access to the very worst parts of his wounds.

As I carefully cut away dead skin, sloughed scabs, and handfuls of hair caked with mud and serum, I couldn't help but wonder if this isn't exactly like those moments when we choose to allow God to come inside and heal us. What a sweet moment of surrender it is when we release a deep sigh and finally turn and reveal our ugliest parts for Him to begin carefully removing all of our "decay." Once our oozing, emotional battleground is exposed and our festering "sensitivities" are carefully cleansed of all that isn't truth… only then is our healing free to come. *Wow, Lord…if only I would stand this still for You during these unpleasant but very necessary times of healing and growth*, I thought to myself as I finished up.

"There, we're all done!" I said to Julie, who was still holding Little Bear's head while grooming him. Together, we marveled at how much larger and deeper the actual injury was…once it was fully exposed. Yet, we both clearly understood that this was the only way to bring about a purposeful healing.

———————||———————

Little Bear's damage was so extensive that his injuries took *nine months* to heal. But heal they did.

Our young colt had survived a bear attack at what was probably only weeks after his birth. He survived being badly injured even while separated from his mother, who was his only source of comfort, protection, and love. With a large, gaping wound, he walked right past the searching eyes of those who were seeking obvious external defects. And in a trailer with dozens of other infants who were healthy and twice his size, he was moved 1,200 miles...without being crushed.

In nearly every aspect of his life today, he stands as one who has both figuratively and in flesh and blood defied what most would consider impossible odds.

When "someone needs to do something" rose up and stood before Virginia and Vicki, they quietly understood that on this day..."someone" was them. They took an unlikely chance on something they believed in with full understanding that what is impossible with man...is possible with God.

True to his heritage, Little Bear now stands close to sixteen hands and weighs in at approximately 1,400 pounds of pure buckskin "play"! Even though his hamstring was compromised by his injury, he has apparently recruited surrounding tissue and remains completely sound.

Today, our "golden boy" still stands as one of the most unique and favored horses among those who come to visit. He is living proof that sometimes what seems unsurvivable...*can* be survived. His life continues to show us that it's okay to push

forward, mud and all, through what is painful…to find genuine healing.

"Genuine healing" now lives on my ranch. Daily he proceeds to emanate gentle truth that encourages those around him to pick themselves up and keep trying…even when the way is dark.

His incredible story of survival calls those who are searching and reminds them that faith, when it is authentic, requires us to act and live in the shadow of what we know is already true.

Real faith begets action. When we acknowledge that everything we do has an effect on someone else, either good or bad, it opens our eyes and shores us up against how easy it is to become lulled into thinking that our actions are really just too small to matter much. We clearly see the consequences that when we choose to do nothing…nothing is what we will reap.

At one time or another, all of us have been in a situation where we heard our own thoughts shouting, *Someone needs to do something here*, or *Someone really needs to step up and help*.

Real faith encourages us that sometimes…*someday* is today, and that *someone*…is you.

———————————||————————————

*Young Wisdom*
_____

Ella, age 4, when calling the horses to the fence:
"Okay, everyone who wants me to pet them…
raise your hands…c'mon, raise 'em up!"

# 5

## Promise Land

All I could do was wonder as I looked at the three-year-old colt that stood before me. As a pale, palomino Appaloosa draped with a long white mane and tail, he was truly a rare and spectacular beauty. Yet my eyes continued to fall to his feet; my perplexity was completely centered on one question: "How can this young man even stand on feet such as these?" I have seen much equine hardship in my years of horse rescue and rehabilitation, but nothing like the four hooves that balanced in front of me.

His pale, almost ethereal golden color stood out in sharp contrast against his hideously purple hooves. It was obvious that not long ago, this youngster sustained such significant trauma to all four of his hoof capsules…that they responded by filling with blood. I could only imagine crushing all of my toenails…then trying to stand on tip-toe. With every searing heartbeat, his pain must have throbbed like unison hammer blows to each hoof.

I ran my hand up under his forelock and rubbed his forehead. Just the thought of such pressurized agony made me wince.

He was owned by a friend of mine who had previously sold the beautiful colt to someone who she thought would provide a good home for him. Sadly, she was wrong.

Like so many other tales of equine woe, even the best of intentions from their human keepers, without good follow-through, are worth less than the time it takes to think them.

It was my understanding that the new owners had "intended" to have the colt's feet trimmed, but never did. Unfortunately for the youngster, his hooves grew out into an abnormally vertical "tin can" shape. His hooves, instead of having a normal forty-five-degree angle from the coronet band (hair line) to the ground, were nearly vertical. All of his natural shock absorbing ability was negated by the new harsh angle above his hooves. Each ankle, instead of gracefully dipping toward the ground with every step, was now forced to thrust straight down, literally "jack-hammering" the hoof capsule with every painful step.

The young horse was finally put out with other adult horses that "ran him down" for several days because he was new to their herd. The colt's resulting injuries caused such severe damage to the inside of his hooves that they had indeed filled with blood.

When my friend was made aware of her former horse's situation, she strongly encouraged the new owners to have a farrier come out and begin rehabilitative trimming immediately. Adding to the young horse's troubles, the new owners thought that "anyone with a pair of nippers" would suffice, and inadvertently employed a backyard butcher! The "farrier" they hired hacked off so much of the colt's foot that he cut into living tissue, causing nearly uncontrollable bleeding from the colt's mutilated feet.

That was more than enough reason for my friend to show up at their ranch, with her trailer in tow, and buy the crippled young colt back.

After knowing all of this, it gave me great surprise when I stepped away from this troubled young spirit…and he followed me! Although he was much improved since his "trim," I was certain that every step was still an effort for him.

In the time that ensued, I thought often of the beautiful, pale colt, always wondering if he was all right, if he was healing well, and if my friend had found a suitable home for him. I smiled to myself, yielding full recognition that this unique young horse had limped his way deep into my heart.

It came as no surprise to me that when a space became available in our horse program, he was the first one that came to my mind to fill it. Only days later, I was settling him into our quarantine paddock.

Karen, a friend of mine, called and described how she was a new volunteer for Sparrow Club and was just beginning to work with a wonderful, very horse-crazy little girl.

It is one of our highest honors to serve those who might need something "extra." We are privileged to partner with other organizations who also strive to fill the void within children who are struggling to cope with circumstances that reach far beyond "normal." One such organization is called Sparrow Club. This unique outreach "adopts" kids that are in medical crisis and raises funds to offset their medical expenses. What is so awe-inspiring about this group is that those who are responsible to raise the financial help are all kids! To my knowledge, this is the only youth-based charity that does this kind of service. Not only does the "sparrow" receive financial support, but perhaps even more important, they receive tangible encouragement, friendship, and love from their peers.

It was explained to me that this child was very sick with an extraordinarily rare disease that primarily attacks the heart. It seems that the illness inhibits the heart's ability to grow along with the child. Ultimately, the child's growth exceeds their struggling heart's capacity to supply blood to their own body. My friend shared with me that the oldest previous survivor of this condition died at the age of nine...our little friend was ten.

After making arrangements for both of them to come to the ranch for a visit, I hung up the phone and just stopped.

It is so easy to be sidetracked by the difficulties in our life and completely miss how incredibly precious every minute is...*every* minute.

Days later, when the ranch was quietly closed, my friend Karen arrived with her young companion. When the little "adopted sparrow" slipped out of the car, from a distance, she looked like every neighbor's little cutie next door. She was beautiful. Her slender frame was topped with wavy blond hair and intense blue eyes. Appropriately, her name was Angelica.

As she approached, every step seemed to carry her farther under a cloak of acute shyness. When she finally stood before me, her timid demeanor prevented her from even looking up.

Together, all three of us walked slowly over to one of the picnic tables on the ranch. Even though she was slightly behind me, I was very aware of how labored her breathing was.

When we reached the table, I chose to sit across from Angelica so I could get to know her a little better before we started our day. Immediately I could see that this was far too much engagement for her. Karen saw it too, and gracefully excused herself, releasing Angelica to perhaps speak more freely.

My new little friend could manage only to look straight down at the table or the ground. All of my questions about her life, her family, her pets were met with a near silent shrug or nod. *How many times has she been through this, Lord?* I wondered, as I continued to observe her fidgeting uneasiness. It was then that I noticed it. Although extremely faint, it was certainly there; encircling her lips was a very pale "halo" of blue.

I didn't know weather this bluish ring was a result of her condition or a response to her rising level of stress. The one thing I did understand was that this type of "communication" between us was not working at all. I needed to shift gears fast.

"Hey, I've been told that you and I have something in common. We are both horse-crazy! I was so glad to hear that about you because I have a young horse that just came to the ranch not long ago, and he is in great need of 'horse-crazy girl love'... do you think you could spare some?"

Her blue eyes began to lift. She did not look at me, but instead looked around for the horse I had just described to her.

"How about if we go to the tack room and get a halter for the new young horse that needs some of your attention?"

At this question, she did look directly at me. It was brief, like a little spark arcing across toward a like conduit. As small as it was, it became the tiny current of commonality between us. Together, we slowly walked toward the tack room to get a halter.

In the short time that my "pale boy" had been at the ranch, he had consistently demonstrated remarkable poise and quietness for such a young horse. He presented more like a much older soul...all except for his relentless curiosity, which drew him like an unseen magnet to explore *everything*.

As we walked into the quarantine paddock, I was pleased to see that he not only turned to face Angelica, but actually took a few steps toward her as well. He was so gentle with her that I chose to allow her to lead him alone. I walked closely behind Angelica to assist her if she needed my help. She didn't.

Although it cost her physically, she seemed pleased that she accomplished the simple chore alone. Once at the hitching post, we retrieved a brush bucket from the barn and began his grooming process. We stood side by side, both brushing the same part of the horse's belly. The rhythmic motion seemed to have a comforting effect on her.

"I love horses…" she volunteered.

With raised brows, I looked at her sideways and smiled. "Me too," I added.

Step by hesitant step, like a little fawn cautiously venturing out into a clearing, she began to speak. If I looked directly at her, she would stop talking. But as soon as I looked straight ahead at our horse, the trickle of words would continue. I was absolutely fascinated by this shy phenomenon.

I shared with Angelica the young horse's story and how much suffering he had endured. Her brushing nearly stopped; she was processing that fact. Maybe she was identifying that they were similar in their paths of pain.

Without looking up she quietly asked, "What's his name?" Her tone and posture indicated that this was vitally important to her.

"He doesn't have one yet. Nearly every horse that comes to the ranch is renamed as a symbolic passage into what we hope will be a better life for them. He is so unique—not only in his story but also his color as well—that he needs a special name. Maybe you can help me name him?"

Now it was her turn to raise her eyebrows and look at me sideways with a little grin.

The little trickle of words had become a steady flow.

After grooming his body, cleaning his hooves, and combing out his silky mane and tail, we had completed our task. An uncertain crossroad split before us. I didn't know how much she was able to do, so instead of asking what she couldn't do, I asked her what she *wanted* to do.

In bewilderment, I watched as her countenance fell back to the ground again. Her small eyebrows furrowed together in what looked like a full-on bar fight between her rising anger and plummeting sorrow. Her colliding emotions mounted until her beautiful face began to show the stress of imminent tears. After what felt like long moments, she finally looked up at me. Her expression embodied pure frustration, anger, and sadness all tangled around a wounded little heart that fully understood how unfair it was that her life was going to be far too short.

It was her eyes that gave her away. The conflict of her illness versus her will raged behind them. Her mortal illness shouted, "I'm sick and it's getting harder and harder to do the things I love!" while her indomitable will shouted back, "Yeah, but I'm just a little kid, and little kids should get to ride little horses! I just want to be like everyone else who has the chance to ride."

The internal balancing act that Angelica had been trying to maintain about her life and her illness completely collapsed into crumbling despair. Her expression shattered into unmistakable brokenness. Without saying a word, the slight upturn of her eyebrows indicated what her pleading heart was truly trying to ask.

In utter helplessness, I watched as her sky blue eyes filled with glass.

Finally, in a voice nearly choked out by unshed tears, she squeaked, "I think I should get to ride."

"Okay," I confirmed, as I glanced across the main yard toward Karen. Because the ranch was so quiet, I was certain that she heard Angelica's request. Her expression clearly registered concern, yet she confirmed Angelica's mother's wish: If she is willing to try, allow her to.

I reached down for Angelica's hand...and she reached up. Hand in hand, we walked into the tack room.

"So, what do you think we should name him?" I tossed out while gathering our tack.

"Hmmmmm, he needs a very special name," she said with a very thoughtful look.

I looked out the window at our young horse and continued "He is such a beautiful color, what would you call gold that soft? I think that he looks like what Heaven might look like…I think he looks like the promised land…don't you?"

I turned toward Angelica just in time to see her head drop as her little face began to crumple under the weight of intense emotion. Immediately I realized my reckless blunder. *Oh Kim, how could you be so clueless!* Without even thinking, I had shoved my little friend right in the direction that she soon might be going. Understandably, it was clear that her child's heart had not yet come to terms with what will be inevitable for us all. I wanted to cry. She wanted to cry. It was such an awkward moment that we just stood together in the tack room looking down toward the floor.

A lonely tear slid down her cheek and dropped off her chin.

There were no words to say. While holding her tack over one arm, I reached down and rested my hand on the back of her bowed head. Her blond waves were so smooth.

I ran my fingers through the baby soft ringlets that had gathered on the back of her neck.

In complete silence, little tear drops began to dot the tack room floor.

Within the faint breeze moving across the ranch, time just seemed to blow away.

As she began to gather herself, I felt her body rise with a shuddering sigh. Then, out of the stillness rose a thin voice that wasn't much more than a whisper: "If I had my own horse…I would name him Promise Land."

Kneeling down before her, I looked up into her flushed face and simply asked, "Do you think Promise Land is the right name for him?"

While catching a tear with her bottom lip, she silently nodded in agreement.

"Well, that's it then! His name is Promise Land," I said, with as much enthusiasm as the moment would bear. In return she gave me a weak smile and began wiping off her face.

"Let me grab his bridle and we'll be good to go," I said, while reaching toward the back wall of the tack room. Angelica had walked out ahead of me onto the small porch. With new resolve she placed her little fists on her hips and leaned forward, nearly shouting, *"Hey, Promise! How d'ya like yer new name?!"*

In moments, we were leading Promise into the round pen. I told her that we were first going to play a game of Hide and Seek. "You need to spend a bit of time rubbing his face, cheeks, and neck, and when I count to twenty, you have to 'hide' somewhere in the round pen, okay?"

Sometimes kids remind me of how literally they apply what adults might ask of them. For, at my request, Angelica turned around and gave Promise the nostril noogie of the century! This is a very sensitive area on all horses, and Angelica carried out what she thought I meant to the very fullest of her capability! She grabbed Promise by the nostrils and began rubbing as if she was trying to start a fire between her palms! I've never counted to twenty so fast in my whole life! God bless that little horse, he stood there for the entire count and didn't move a foot. When Angelica stepped away from him to go hide, I was certain his muzzle would be either hairless, smoking, or bleeding! Promise took it all like a man and was apparently none the worse for wear because of it.

Angelica skipped about ten steps away, curled up in a little ball, and cupped her hands over her eyes.

"No fair, peeking," I said from behind the gate by the round pen wall. She sat so utterly still that it appeared she was nearly holding her breath.

Promise's head lowered nearly to the ground as he looked in her direction. With several slow, deliberate steps, he closed the gap between them until his chapped nose touched her back. The instant she turned around and saw her new golden friend, she looked at me with an expression of pure, astonished wonder. "Did you *teach* him to do that?" she asked with an incredulous tone.

"No…I didn't. He did that because he wanted to. I think he likes you."

Caught in utter amazement, Angelica's little mouth fell open as her gaze bounced between the horse and me. It was delightfully obvious that the wonder of this little horse choosing her friendship was taking a moment to find its way into her overwhelmed heart.

"Angelica…do you think he really meant it? Let's find out for sure. Do it again," I encouraged. I watched in absolute elation as over and over she "hid" from the little horse as he over and over sought her out for love. The building wonder and enthusiasm on her face was enough to fuel my jets for another ten years.

Finally, she asked if she could ride him.

With full understanding of his history, I acknowledged that she was a very small, very special girl. Leading him around at a walk, with her on his back, would certainly do them both some good.

With great care, I lifted Angelica up onto his back. After

a few simple instructions, we were off. I led Promise as she "steered." We had just made one full lap of the round pen when Angelica began to gasp for breath. With one hand pressed to her chest, she looked at me and mouthed, "I'm done."

I looked back to see that the faint "bluishness" around her lips was now taking over her whole face. Immediately I dropped the lead rope and scooped her off his back. As I carried her out of the round pen, I asked, "Angelica, what do you need?" Her response was a weak, "I need to lie down."

I handed her off to Karen, who was nearly as white as Angelica, and quickly dragged a picnic table over into the shade. Together, Karen and I helped her lie down on the heavy wooden bench.

I sat with Angelica as she continued to gasp. In dismay, I watched as her whole body slowly turned white.

Karen rushed to her car and pounded out a "911" to Angelica's mother on her cell phone. While Karen spoke to the girl's mother in the distance, I wondered, *Lord, is this it? Is this precious little Angelica now going home?* Kneeling beside her in the grass, I threaded my fingers between hers and quietly held her hand.

Slowly, seemingly everything in the world silently returned to normal. Karen came back with news from Angelica's mother that some days are better than others and occasionally, when her daughter is excited or tired, this happens.

As Angelica stabilized, I left Karen with her for a moment to retrieve some juice and snacks from our home. Angelica was still curled into a fetal position on the bench when I returned. She was beginning to brighten a bit, but remained lying on her side. After settling the snacks on the table above her head, I went into the round pen to rescue Promise, who was standing at the gate looking for his friend.

His presence had brightened her before...perhaps he could do it again. I led my little blond boy over onto the grass near Angelica and dropped his rope.

Although he was free to graze, wander, or do whatever young horses wish to do...he chose to stand fast. Instead of satisfying his own instinctive needs by grazing, his intentions were fixed only on Angelica. Repeating what he had just done in the round pen, he took slow and deliberate steps toward the recovering girl.

As if not to wake her, he stretched his golden neck to its full length, and with the speed of a setting sun, slowly lowered his chin until it rested on her temple. Because he was above her, she did not see his approach and she did, indeed, startle.

"Oh! It's you," she said, when she realized who was touching her. Then, she completely relaxed beneath the contact of his muzzle.

Once again, I stood in complete amazement of the simple awareness of a young horse to a young girl. All horse owners know that all horses graze all the time. That's what horses do...all but *this* horse. He seemed to understand, and chose instead to stand guard over a very sick child who needed him more than he needed to fill his belly with grass.

Before me stood a young recovering horse standing guard over a young recovering girl. It seemed as if our roles had now reversed. Now it was I who could only watch in pure, astonished wonder while thinking, *Did you teach him to do that?* No...he did it because he wanted to. He must really like her a lot!

It was now my turn to stand in near slack-jawed amazement as this glorious wonder found its way into my heart.

# 6

## *Full Circle*

Aspecial call came in mid-November. It was Brenda, a dear friend. As a parent, I have told her that she ranks in my book as a superstar. Yet, in typical Bren fashion, she only rolls her eyes and makes some self-deprecating comment like, "If you only knew! Just ask my kids, they'll tell you what a *star* I am!"

I not only love Bren because she loves her own kids, which one would easily expect…I also deeply admire her because she leads the way in loving those children who can be a challenge to love. Not only does she have three of her own children, she also has three adopted children and has been a temporary mother to many more foster children. I am constantly amazed at how easily she weaves the lives of hurting children in and around her own kids' lives and encourages both to change each other for the better. Truly, she is one of the most heroic and selfless women I know.

As Brenda began speaking, I could immediately hear that her easy-going manner was strained. Her normal "roll with the punches" outlook sounded stretched and thin. Concern rose in my chest for my friend as she began our conversation with "I need to ask you for a favor…"

After a long and convoluted explanation, I clearly understood why her voice sounded so "tight." She had explained to me how her family had taken in a small, six-year-old boy, Jason, and his infant half sister. They were received into their home in September after their single mother was incarcerated.

The situation was further complicated by the fact that Jason's mother, though having never been married, had children with several different men. Therefore, the tiny half sister was released two months later to her biological father. And even though this "father" named Andy truly loved Jason and was the only "dad" that he had ever known…Jason could not go home with him because he was not his biological father and he had no legal right to be involved in his life outside the presence of his mother. Sadly, Andy was just another man who had moved into—and out of—Jason's life. Unfortunately, at that time, the whereabouts of Jason's real father was unknown.

Brenda continued to explain how, on that cool September afternoon, a little boy and his tiny sister were brought to her home—complete strangers—and left. In a heart-demolishing moment, the only dad the boy knew came and picked up the baby sister…and drove away without him. In an instant, Brenda's brand new six-year-old foster son had lost his mother, his "father," and the only sister he had. All those he knew to be his family, in his eyes, were gone…forever.

As Brenda spoke, I realized that I knew this child. I had met him once before while bumping into the family in a local grocery store. What I remembered most about him were his eyes. Like many kids, he possessed beautiful blue eyes, but what set him apart were his eyelashes. In all my life, on either adult or child, I had never seen such magnificent eyelashes. They were so remarkably long that they brushed not only his cheeks…but his brows as well.

Brenda shared with me how he had mournfully cried, grieving his incredible loss for many nights, and woke up an equal number of mornings in a wet bed. Day by day this broken child began to come to terms with the truth that his life would never be the same.

Within the safety and love of Brenda and her family, Jason slowly began to emerge. His shy expression melted into a smile and gradually into boyish play. Bit by loving bit, the little boy started to rise in the morning with a subtly renewed confidence…and a dry bed.

Incredibly, within this highly fractured family, Jason's maternal grandparents were located and began to show great involvement with their grandson. After he spent many fun-filled outings with them, his grandparents made it openly known to all that their intentions were to obtain legal guardianship of Jason. Being in their forties, they were still young and had decided that they could give him a loving, stable, and permanent home. Jason was overjoyed.

Brenda continued Jason's tale of woe by observing how his new horizon of hope was crushed beyond recognition when the grandparents realized it was possible that their daughter, Jason's mom, might eventually be released from jail and want to reclaim him—which would be a complicated, emotional bridge that they did not wish to cross. Almost as suddenly as they entered his life, Jason's grandparents exited. To say that Jason was distraught might be the same as saying it smarts a little to be run over by a train. Brenda recounted how his sense of rejection and devastation reached a new and overwhelming low.

Because of the constant love that surrounded him, Jason fought like a drowning child, once again, struggling to reach the surface of his own life.

After many weeks, Brenda was contacted by Jason's case worker. Miraculously, his biological father had now been found. Through a messy tangle of circumstances, Travis had become separated from his son and had been searching for him for many years. He had full understanding that his son would not remember him and that Jason had since been cared for by many men who had stepped into the role of "father." Travis made it clear that he wished to re-enter his son's life as gently as possible and hopefully become the family that Jason needed most.

The case worker had arranged a neutral meeting in ten days.

Brenda continued her sad saga by relating how both she and the case worker agreed that they would not put Jason's heart through another trial of "high hopes" only to have them trampled again. If Jason were to safely meet his biological father, it would be best for his tender heart if his father's identity was not revealed to him until they were sure that Jason felt comfortable and safe within Travis's presence.

Initially, Brenda related that the case worker was going to set up the meeting within a bowling alley because it was a fun and open, kid-friendly place. But Bren, knowing the true depth of Jason's loss and continued suffering, understood that this environment was too noisy and too public if Jason needed a safe retreat. She intuitively knew that Jason required a place to go where meeting a stranger wouldn't be so strange. "Kim...can we set up the meeting at the ranch?" was her true reason for calling.

I was grateful that the appointed day for Jason to meet his real father fell on an afternoon when the ranch was closed. Coming over on her day off, Sandy, who was part of the ranch staff, volunteered to help me with this very tenuous encounter. She offered to bring out an extra horse so that Brenda's older kids could also ride in the arena, and this might make the day feel more "natural."

Before Brenda and her family arrived, a strange car pulled into the ranch's main yard. From it exited a very nervous young man and his mother. I introduced myself to Travis, Jason's father, and to his grandmother, and tried to make them feel as comfortable as possible. I knew that they both lived in Idaho and neither had seen Jason in approximately five years. Together they had driven a great distance and must surely be exhausted…both physically and emotionally. In an effort to relieve their understandable anxiety, I invited them both to join me across the driveway to meet some of our baby horses. As we scratched the young horses, many silent prayers rose for the outcome of this extremely fragile day. It was very apparent that not only was a child's heart in peril of being destroyed…but his father's heart as well.

The case worker soon arrived, and not long afterward Brenda's van also pulled into the yard. To help camouflage and "normalize" the meeting, Brenda wisely decided to bring four of her older kids along with Jason. Not wishing to set him up for a heart break, Brenda shared only that there would be a few "others" at the ranch as well. Immediately, with the acute sensitivity that only a foster child can have, his apprehension began to rise with the very real awareness that he might be abandoned with strangers once again. Brenda, realizing his rising fear, quickly followed with, "Hey, it's really cold today. How about when we *all* get home, we will *all together* make hot chocolate with marshmallows…" Although visibly relieved, Jason knew something was up.

*Lord, this is it; please help heal what is left of this family…* I prayed as I gently moved a very nervous young man and his equally tense mother toward the lost remnant of what was once a family.

Introductions flew back and forth in a tangled jumble of words, handshakes, and hugs. Everyone but Jason was acutely aware of the incredible impact that the next few moments would hold.

I watched him as he looked up into the face of the man who was his real father…with absolutely no recognition at all. I could not even begin to imagine the shattering pain raining down within Travis's heart at that moment. Travis bent down, took his sunglasses off and gently introduced himself.

I could hardly believe what I was seeing once this man's sunglasses were removed…there were revealed the most incredibly blue eyes…framed by the longest eyelashes I had ever seen. They, too, not only brushed his cheeks…but his brows as well. Wonder totally enveloped me as I watched near mirror images greet each other face to face.

Sandy took Brenda's kids and began tacking up Jasmine, an older, gray Appaloosa mare. I invited Travis to join Jason, Nathan (the youngest of Brenda's kids), and me as we groomed and tacked up Teva, a wonderfully short and sweet palomino mare.

My own concerns for Travis began to rise as I became acutely aware of his sudden pallor transformation. His skin tone seemed to be changing quite suddenly from an adrenalized flushed pink to a clammy white. After politely excusing himself, Travis seemed to be spending more time behind the round pen than with our little gathering at the hitching post. I wasn't certain, but within such an emotionally charged environment, I wouldn't have been surprised if he was throwing up.

Travis had been made aware that his lost son's life had been disastrous. He understood that as much as he wanted to, he could not rush in and scoop up his son in a flurry of kisses. Though he ached to, he could not say, "Hey, I'm your dad, I love you, and I'm taking you home with me." He acknowledged that in order for this meeting to be "processed" by Jason…he had to go slow and wait for the right moment.

As the two little boys and I led Teva out into the arena, Jason looked up at me with a small furrow between his brows. "I've never ridden a horse before," he admitted in a very quiet voice. He was afraid. "We're okay; how 'bout if Nathan rides first so that you can see for yourself how lovable Teva is?" I replied in a voice that I hoped would give him comfort.

Since Nathan had ridden before, I was a little surprised when he also was a bit hesitant. It was clear that the best thing to do was settle him in the saddle and just stand quiet for a moment. I invited Travis to come out into the arena and walk on the off side of Teva as I led her, just so that Nathan would feel "extra safe."

It didn't occur to me until several laps later, when Nathan was calling and waving to everyone that would wave back, that this truly was the perfect scenario for Jason to get to know his dad.

"Okay, now it's Jason's turn," I announced from the arena as I helped a triumphant Nathan down the mounting block.

I watched as Jason made his way through the arena's sand. His helmeted little head was down and his demeanor looked as if he had just been asked to "walk the plank." Fear clung to him like his small, rumpled coat.

As I helped Jason climb to the top of the mounting block, I explained to him that he could step across onto the saddle when he felt like he was ready, and that all together we would stand still for as long as he wished.

There, on the top of the mounting block, Jason stood as frozen as a statue.

I could only guess at what must have been going through his head. I wondered if within his mighty contemplation he was considering how much this paralleled his life...stepping out into the unfamiliar...to do the unthinkable...with the unknown.

Jason's father was standing on the other side of the horse. Jason studied the saddle for some time...then looked across into the face of his father...and reached out.

Within that moment of catching his son, I am certain that Travis was intensely grateful for his sunglasses. While trying to balance on the high wire of what he needed to do...and what he wanted to do, Travis was nearly as stiff as a wooden soldier.

The thinly veiled emotion of everyone involved was beginning to crack.

To ease Jason's fears, I asked him a barrage of simple questions. In no time he began to relax, and our trio set off to circle the arena.

As Jason became more confident, I rotated my attention to Travis. As with his son, I wished to relieve his tension by asking him easy questions about what he loved. After Travis had spoken freely about many things, it was as simple as a child's game to "connect the dots." "Wow! Travis likes to hike. Jason, I bet that you like to hike too! Travis thinks that swimming is pretty fun. Jason, what do you think? Do you like to swim?"

With tentative steps, father and son began to cross the newly forged bridge that lay between them. Slowly, they started speaking directly to each other.

As we came around by the arena gate, I looked into Travis's

face and smiled. He understood my expression when I silently passed Teva's lead rope to him and walked away. My arms prickled with anticipated hope as behind me...a gentle verbal "rainbow" was beginning to take shape. I could hear the first, soft-spoken bonds starting to form between a father and his boy.

After many laps together, punctuated with animated gestures, stories, and even a bit of muted laughter, Travis led Teva and Jason up to the fence where the rest of us had gathered. With Sandy and the older kids trotting raucous laps in the background, the case worker indicated to Brenda that she thought it was time...time for Jason to be told the truth about this new "friend" that he was beginning to trust.

With every step that Brenda took toward Jason, I could sense tension rising within all of the adults. So much was at risk. So much damage had already been done. Both father and son had already suffered so greatly. What would happen if Jason broke, if he refused to accept this "nice guy" as his father? Could this young father bear another moment of not embracing the lost son that inexcusable circumstances had stolen from him?

While sitting nearby on the arena fence, I felt like my chest was so brittle that if I took a breath, it might splinter into a million pieces. I could not begin to understand what Travis's heart must have felt like. *Lord...we need Your help...*

With undeniable courage, Brenda stopped on the opposite side of Teva. She took a deep breath and looked directly into Jason's eyes. His expression began to change; he knew that something big was coming.

"Honey, I know that you understand that 'Andy' was your dad, and he took good care of you and your little sister. But when your mom went away, Andy couldn't take both of you because, you remember, he was not your birth dad. Before Andy, your mom knew another man and you were born. Then your mom knew Andy, and then your sister was born."

Brenda paused for this gentle reminder to firm up within Jason's memory. "Honey, remember earlier today when you met Travis? Do you remember looking at his eyes?" At this mention, Travis silently removed his sunglasses. "Jason, his eyes are blue and look just like your eyes…"

Jason turned and openly stared at Travis.

Travis's shoulders were forward, his chin was low, his hands were in front of him literally "white knuckling" the lead rope. Everything about his posture was pleading for his son to accept him…as his father.

Jason turned back toward Brenda and with childlike innocence stated, "Andy's eyes are also blue…" Brenda continued with gentle grace, "Yes, Andy's eyes are a beautiful blue as well, and he loves you very much…but Travis's eyes look like yours…because they *are* yours. You see, Andy is the dad who raised you, but Travis is the dad who *made* you. The same blood inside him is the same blood that is inside you." Jason's attempt to process this new information showed as his eyes slowly moved from staring at Travis's face…to staring at the blood that pulsed within his wrists.

Brenda cautiously moved on. "Travis remembers you. He remembers holding you when you were a baby, and loving you very, very much. He has been looking for you for a long time…and now he has found you. Travis wants to keep on loving you…because he is your dad. Do you think that would be okay? Travis would like to come to *our house* and visit you. He loves you Jason…and he doesn't ever want to lose you again."

Jason continued to stare at Travis. Again, his small eyebrows came together as he fought to understand exactly who this nice man was that stood before him. Finally, Jason looked back toward Brenda with a surprisingly relaxed expression. Apparently, he had decided that everything she had shared was okay with him.

Brenda closed by saying, "Travis is the daddy who made you...and as you choose, he would like to become your friend. And when you are ready to choose him as your dad...Travis wants to become the daddy that will raise you. Honey, do you understand?"

Jason answered her question with a weak nod.

"Jason, do you want to have Travis lead you around the arena again so that you can talk?"

Jason's expression softened slightly as he thought about this suggestion, and again he replied with a wordless nod.

I was in complete awe. Even though I have the privilege of observing it often, I am always completely amazed at the resilient heart of a child. It appeared as if the veil between them was, thread by thread, being torn in half. The film of uncertainty surrounding each of them was beginning to lift like a vapor.

A little boy abandoned...then fostered. Once an orphan... now a son. A child without family...takes the hand of his father. The boy once lost...was now found.

Truth and time...are like that. Combined together, they form a sieve that eventually sifts away all that is not genuine.

I watched in awe as together father and son circled the arena over...and over...and over. Like ruts in a familiar, well-traveled dirt road, each revolution seemed to further entrench the new truth growing between them. I could see that once again, as with their earlier laps around the arena, the animation, the stories, and the soft laughter rose from their combined company.

Relief, joy, love, and "completeness" mulled together in a powerful combination, reflecting the desires of everyone on the ranch. All those present saw how the healing love of a foster family had become the literal stepping stone of reconciliation and support for time to *prove* what is true.

We all need to be needed, to be special to someone…to become part of a family. Watching father and son choose to become united inspired my own gratitude to rise on the wings of thanksgiving for the "family," both blood and chosen, that God has provided in my life.

In a different way, in a different time, in a different voice… someone once did something similar for me—by reaching through what might have looked like impossible odds and inviting me to become part of their family…and it saved my life. The "baton" of parenthood had been passed within my life, and I was glad that I was able to be a small part of this "passing" for another.

The path of hoofprints leading around the arena seemed to become much more than just a symbolic reminder that within my heart also… a "full circle" had been made.

# 7

## Fruits and Vegetables

Rachel, who is the Volunteer Coordinator for Crystal Peaks, shared with me a unique conversation that she recently had with a child who was visiting the ranch.

Upon seeing someone that she did not recognize, the little girl asked Rachel in a purely inquisitorial fashion, "Who is that man over there?" Rachel looked in the direction of her inquiry and answered, "Oh, that's Allan. He's a 'Kiwi' from New Zealand. He has a wonderful voice…you should go and talk to him so you can hear how beautiful his accent is."

Armed with such a delightful suggestion, the little one set out to discover what a "Kiwi" sounded like.

Rachel recounted that a short time later the little girl returned to the group in apparent triumph. She bravely declared to all her friends, "That man over there's name is Allan. He sounds so neat…you should go and talk to him, because he's…ahhh, ahhh, a… Zucchini!"

# 8

# Simply... Step Up

Darkness had already overwhelmed the weakened daylight of December. It was early evening, and Troy and I were in our bedroom and just beginning to pack for a five-day trip. We had been eagerly anticipating the six-hour drive together to the Steens Mountain wilderness simply to just get caught up. In the high desert of southeastern Oregon, the region where we make camp is so remote that it greatly facilitates a time of restoration, refilling, and concentration for the work projects that had to be completed during this time. Even though our laptops were going with us, we were still so excited for our mini-getaway.

I had just separated out all of the super-warm clothing that I intended to pack, when the phone rang.

The call for help came from a frantic-sounding volunteer who had just been appointed as a volunteer coordinator by the Deschutes County Sheriff's Department. Within moments, I felt like I was being buried alive under her avalanche of desperate information. Scribbling wildly, I tried to record the incredulous report that was pouring like an icy flood through the phone. As I listened, I noticed that I was physically shaking my head no. I realized that my heart seemed to be rejecting all that poured into my ear. I didn't *want* to believe, *couldn't* believe that these atrocities were true.

Apparently, the Sheriff's Department had confirmed that just east of Bend, there was a large herd of horses in critical need. During one of the most frigid months of the year, these horses were largely without food or water. Many of them had hooves so long that they could barely move. Others were so desperately thin that emergency care would surely be needed. It was currently estimated that the needy herd involved more than *one hundred* horses…and counting.

We were officially requested by the Sheriff's Department to help give aid in moving this starving mob. The volunteer on the phone continued by making it very clear that most of these horses had rarely seen a human being—and certainly had never been touched by one.

The location we were called to was approximately twenty-five miles east of Bend. It was just beyond a roadside gas station that was the only indication of a miniscule town called Millican. From this time-forgotten landmark, the actual rescue sight was about eight miles further east into the windswept hills of the high desert.

Summoned to join a team of many other volunteers, Troy and I would be pulling out before dawn.

Our packing screeched to a halt and our overnight bags were left open on the bed as Troy and I stepped out into the bitter darkness to load and hitch our horse trailer. Our time of rest would have to wait. For now, only a few hours of sleep separated us from what would become the largest horse rescue in Oregon's history.

Within the pre-daylight hours, an ice fog had cast its frigid cape over the land, covering all in a thick, translucent garment of ice. Merely driving in these conditions was hazardous. Many would consider pulling a horse trailer in such treacherous weather as bordering on suicidal behavior. Driving no more than twenty miles an hour, with both hands firmly gripping the wheel, Troy drove as if he had no steering or brakes. When traveling over such heavy ice, the reality is that you truly have neither. With a heavy trailer behind us, it was tenuous going at best.

Nearly an hour and a half later, we were grateful to turn off the dangerously icy highway and onto a rutted dirt road. With no trees, buildings, or other signs of life in sight, the road seemed to wind aimlessly through the hills toward some forgotten place.

As we crested the top of a small rise, the fog had lifted enough to reveal an illusive image in the distance. Dozens of parked horse trailers emerged like a mirage from the desert floor. The newly appointed herald had apparently done her job well, as had the dozens of ranchers who were contacted and who chose to respond with immediate compassion on such a treacherous day.

In the feeble light of morning, we followed the lead of those who had come before us and parked in an organized diagonal pattern out in the frozen sage. Looking back through the fog in the direction that we had just traveled, I could see the approaching headlights of more rigs on the way.

I stepped out of the warmth of the truck into air so frigid that my breath seemed to shatter like white glass before me. With a deep shudder, I slipped on my hat and gloves and met Troy at the front of the truck. Side by side, we walked together toward a large gathering of heavily bundled folks.

As we walked hand in hand, the remnants of trash came into view. Reams of snarled barbed wire lay partially up and mostly down in what appeared to have been a fence at one time. Perhaps fifty to sixty people were milling around between completely dilapidated makeshift "corrals" that looked to hold between one to three horses each.

Even before entering the crowd, I could feel everyone's combined anxious tension from our distance. *What are we walking into?* I wondered. As the hairs on the back of my neck began to hackle, I simply asked, *Lord, be our strength, wisdom, and peace...*

I could see maybe six uniformed deputies surrounding one lieutenant from the Sheriff's Department who appeared to be trying to organize what to do next. Everyone talked at once, and the lieutenant was trying, amidst a cloud of rising stress, to locate a place where these horses, who were all in desperate need, could be relocated.

From the deputy standing next to me, I learned that a middle-aged couple—who were now under arrest—had lived on this site for four years. During this time, the number of their horse herd had exploded to a staggering *130* horses! No wonder the rescuers were having so much trouble finding a suitable location. Most rescue facilities, ranches, or private homes were equipped to handle only a few extra horses in need...not 130!

The only known facility large enough to handle a herd this size was more than one hundred miles away, and was equipped to handle only "healthy" horses. Further complicating the problem, this location was well over a hundred miles away from those who could provide continuing care for these neglected horses.

Breaking up this critical herd into dozens of smaller groups spread over several counties was not an option either. Not only were these horses needing specialized care, they were also being held as "evidence" in a pending investigation. And—most limiting of all—they were completely wild.

I couldn't help but notice the unmistakable sound of desperation in the voice of the deputy who spoke to me. No county in the state of Oregon had ever attempted an equine rescue of this magnitude before. There were no previous examples to follow, there were no guidelines, and currently... there were no suitable locations to house this starving mass.

According to the deputy, there were no less than thirty horses who needed to be moved to an intensive care center immediately. The remaining hundred, although in dire condition, needed to be moved to a facility that could accommodate continuing first-aid measures, vaccinations and deworming, hoof care, and safe fencing. These horses included several dozen adult stallions, several adult mares who nearly all appeared pregnant, and about fifty sub-adult colts and fillies.

Now, it became clear why the deputies felt such incredible pressure. Here were 130 starving, wild horses turned over into their care...and as of yet, they had nowhere to properly care for them.

As I began to fully comprehend the severity, complexity, and sheer magnitude of this rescue, each aspect felt like a separate stone falling into my heart.

Everyone was here to help...yet, without a safe location and a plan, there was nothing the assembled group of volunteers could do.

Many, in an effort to help, offered various ideas that ultimately all sounded something like, "Let's move the entire herd to 'so-and-so' field until we can find something better." It was clear that their intentions, although kind, did not fully consider that these were not "normal" horses, but *wild* horses that could not be touched. Just moving them once was going to be an *extremely* dangerous affair. Not to mention fencing, vetting, and adult stallions attempting to kill each other...

Unfortunately, with so many offering partial solutions at the same time, the result seemed less like help and more like a verbal firing line to the assaulted officer. A barrage of cell phone ring tones cluttered the air even more as they all seemed to compete for attention. Like a hapless grade school band warming up, voices rose in conflict and contest against each other.

While Troy paused beside the lieutenant, who was acting as the incident commander, to hopefully glean some information, I walked on beyond the crush to evaluate the situation.

I am not certain that I could have spoken even if I wanted to, as there were just no words to describe the overwhelming amount of sheer squalor that filled my eyes. While slowly passing through row after row of haphazard horse "pens," abandoned fencing, collapsed sheds, and discarded black plastic bags of trash gutted out everywhere, I came upon the first horse. She was loose, wandering aimlessly around looking for something to eat. When she saw my approach, she slowly moved away. She was a very tall, chestnut, thoroughbred-looking type. She was in much pain, judging by the way she moved on her front feet. She walked as if she was trying to balance on an egg with each step. Adding to her sorrows was the fact that she was missing at least three hundred pounds.

I had been walking for what felt like a short distance when the morning fog began to lift. All my previous years of equine rescue did not, *could not,* prepare my heart for what lay ahead.

Approximately thirty horses had been singled out into "pens." Some of these enclosures were no larger than our truck.

As I had been told earlier, the husband and wife who were under investigation for this atrocity, had lived on the property for four years, and it was clear that these penned horses were standing in a four-year accumulation of their own waste. Because they were denied any natural movement on an abrasive surface, their hooves had grown into what looked like grotesque ram's horns that curled up and backwards nearly into their own knees.

Of these, some were blind, most were lame, all were starving. Some walked on the front of their coronet bands instead of the soles of their hooves. Others had legs so twisted with deformity that one might expect hidden wires were holding them up. Just gazing at these haunted creatures…looking into their empty eyes…made my gut tighten with sorrow.

I noticed that several other people had gathered around an area up ahead. As I approached the corral where they stood, I could see that it housed a poor horse with particularly gruesome, overgrown hooves. I felt my body pull in a deep breath of sadness. I quietly remembered that someone wiser than I once said, "There is nothing stronger in this world than the heart of a volunteer." With that resolve firmly in place, I steadied my emotions and raised my camera to document the case. Without warning, the camera was almost slapped out of my hands by an onlooker who nearly screamed at me that I had no authority to take photographs of such a scene. I was so stunned by her demanding and aggressive behavior that I silently obliged her by slipping my camera back into my pocket. Like her, each one of us seemed to be "slapped off balance" by the sheer carnage of what filled our eyes.

Information scattered through the volunteers like white-hot sparks blowing off an abandoned fire. Although there were many faces I did not recognize, most I had seen before. One older rancher, who I knew only casually, stood with his hands buried deep within his worn coat pockets. He had arrived very early and shared with me what he had learned from the lieutenant in charge. He recounted how four years prior, the middle-aged couple fled to this area after being charged with horse abuse in the state of Washington. They moved to this remote sight to start their future herd in seclusion. Within a short amount of time, they were able to secretly acquire roughly twenty horses to start their "retirement" herd. Their unseemly horses consisted of the rejected—old, injured, or behaviorally dangerous—horses from local auctions, race tracks, and equine meat buyers.

It appeared that most of the adult stallions had been kept in the tiny pens, while all of the male offspring ran wild within the rapidly growing herd. It seemed as if the offending couple hadn't bothered to separate out the colts for four years, ensuring that every male horse born on the property was left an intact stallion capable of breeding any female old enough to be in estrus. The breeding "program" was completely unattended. This rag-tag herd had been left to field-breed at will, so sons were breeding their mothers, brothers were breeding their sisters, and fathers were breeding their own daughters. Many fillies had been impregnated before they were even two years of age, fully three years earlier than what most would consider a suitable time for them to safely conceive. The milling, destitute horses before me had grown into a herd of more than one hundred starving souls.

There was more.

I could see that the dwelling being occupied by the couple was no more than a steel travel trailer. Holes in the walls where windows had once been were now boarded up in a primitive effort to prevent the bitter wind, which was now beginning to

blow, from entering their living space. I was told that they did
not have conventional power or water either. A generator was
needed to provide electricity to start up the water pump which
would, in turn, fill the meager plumbing with water…until the
generator shut off again.

Many of us looked to the horses. How long had it been
since they had been offered a drink of water? Even in frigid
conditions, the average horse needs at least five gallons of fresh
water a day—in this case…multiplied by 130!

Slowly circling back toward the main area where the deputies had gathered, I learned even more about what needed
to happen. The task at hand was monumental for the overwhelmed animal control division of the Sheriff's Department.
Slowly they began to organize themselves with chosen volunteers and branch out into areas of immediate need. The horses
were desperate for water, so a small team set out to see what
they could do to remedy the situation.

We learned that the couple also had acquired several working
dogs that were likewise "field breeding." An estimated sixty dogs
were reported to be living in a nameable mountain of garbage.
Another tenacious team was sent head-first into the enormous
heap of trash to retrieve them.

Frantic canine mothers barked nervously as, one by one,
officers and volunteers pulled their beautiful black and white
puppies from dens burrowed deep within the waste.

I walked to the "catch truck" where all the captured puppies were being held. As I approached, every air hole filled with
a tiny nose that sniffed wildly to perhaps catch a scent of their
elusive mothers. Cautiously, I held my flat palm up to one little
nose. To my surprise, the black nose was replaced by a little
pink tongue that began to wash my hand. Casting my caution

aside, I pushed two of my fingers through the hole and began to rub the head of my frightened new little friend.

Staying until another officer returned to the truck, I asked if any of the dogs were in need of a home. He assured me that with nearly miraculous speed, they already had homes waiting...for *all* of them.

Continuing my evaluation of the scene, I moved on past the gigantic pile of trash and dogs, the couple's battered travel trailer, and the tiny pens imprisoning horses mired within their own manure.

The main herd beckoned like a sickening song. The enormity of what loomed before me was staggering. It was becoming more difficult to make my mind focus on such hideous sights as they continued to multiply like a revolting swarm.

While picking my way through trash, rotting lumber, and collapsed fencing, I noticed something else...something unspeakable. Their unmistakable presence shouted in silence of unfathomable horror and suffering—there were...bones...*everywhere.*

*Dear Lord, how many have died here?*

Like somber witnesses of what could be kept secret no longer, a myriad of dull bones, scattered as far as I could see, began to murmur the truth of what really happened here.

As the starving horses collapsed in death...the starving dogs devoured their flesh.

Overwhelming sorrow poured down my spine like ice water. My entire chest tightened with the realization of such horrific carnage.

The fog was continuing to lift. The heavy gray light of morning seemed to join the frozen earth and groan in mourning for these lost ones.

But the worst was still before me.

Troy had made his way from the crush of people toward the main herd as well. In silence, we met at the makeshift gate which was nothing more than two poles caught in a twisted ream of barbed wire. After passing through, we spread out to cover more area. The entire scene was unspeakable, unthinkable, incomprehensible.

Every horse I examined was a new example of the various stages of suffering. Even though they were nearly all young, most wore the expression of those who have seen and known much anguish, like broken souls returning home from war. None were approachable; all moved away with wary, rolling eyes. Eyes that futilely searched the earth for something, anything, to fill the yawning emptiness within.

.    The area that encompassed the main herd of horses was enormous. I could not see the perimeter fencing in any direction. My best guess was that the herd was pressing against the area closest to the vicinity of the pens, trash, and "house" because they were thirsty. Troy and I continued walking. The milling mass of horses opened and closed like phantoms around us as we drifted through their midst. Having seen nearly all I could take, I looked back at Troy. There, standing amongst a sea of ragged, serrated spines, Troy returned and held my gaze. His handsome face was streaked with compassion. Without speaking a word, he heavily raised his arm and pointed.

I looked in the direction he indicated…and could not believe what my eyes saw.

As the horses parted before my hesitant steps, only thirty feet away stood the embodiment of the living dead. Gripped by horror, I could not move another step. She was the most grotesque creature I have ever seen. I could hardly breathe. She was later confirmed as a two-and-a-half-year-old thoroughbred quarter-horse cross. In the world known by most, this cross-breeding produces a towering, muscular horse. At this age, most would stand between fifteen and sixteen hands and weigh well over one thousand pounds. Yet in this forsaken wasteland, she didn't even reach thirteen hands and her life looked to be vanishing nearly as quickly as the morning fog. The wasted filly's total body weight was estimated at *less* than four hundred pounds!

Never have I known a horse in this condition to live.

I have held a horse in better condition…that died in my arms.

Her skeletal body was so parched and drawn that she looked more like an ancient mummy than a young horse. It appeared as if one could nearly span her haunches with their open bare hands. Her top-line was lifted above her body by a spine that resembled uniformly spaced daggers, each threatening to pierce the thin flesh that it supported. Her weakness was so extensive that she appeared to not be able to bend any of her joints. What remained of her utterly withered muscle structure was so frail, it looked as if she were to bend her knees, she might not have enough strength to stop herself from crashing to the ground. There was evidence on her knees, shoulders and chest of where this had already happened countless times.

In my many years of equine rescue I have seen numerous horses grow unnatural body hair in a desperate, eleventh-hour effort to maintain their core temperature, but this horse's lanugo was unlike *anything* I had ever witnessed before. Her hair, instead of being straight like a normal horse, had become nappy and wool-like. Its rampant growth was even invading her mouth, nostrils, and eyes. Sadly, her desperate efforts to stay warm were not supported with enough fuel to work.

Consequently, she had many patches on her back where her skin had literally frozen off. Even from my distance, I could easily smell the stench emanating from her rotting back.

There she stood, emaciated beyond comprehension, balancing on pencilly legs so stiff that her minimal movements resembled more that of a tin man than of a young horse. Would she have enough strength to be moved? Could she survive one more night? Would she be the next to collapse into oblivion?

Tears were dropping off my jaw onto my heavy coat. All I could think of was Mercy. She was a similarly starved, pregnant mare that we had rescued a few years earlier. Immediately I was overcome by the memory of the last moments of holding her head...as she finally gave up her struggle to live. *Dear Lord, my precious Mercy. Not again...please, Lord...not again.* The memory of her death rolled over me like a crushing boulder of sorrow. My heart splintered into immeasurable fragments of grief. Standing in the presence of this dying little soul yanked me back to the moment when Mercy gave up her life in my arms. She suffered immeasurably more than any creature should have to endure. For long moments I wept in silence.

Grief can be like a thunderstorm—blue sky suddenly giving way to black. We can be caught off guard by the hurt of what we have seen, what we have felt. Mourning has consumed many of us in a crashing downpour of pain.

*Please, Lord; with this little one...show me what to do...*

Thankfully, heaven's blue is permanent...grief's dark clouds are not. Gradually, if we hold fast and keep standing, our grief-blackened skies will once again give way to the enduring blue.

With new resolve, I wiped my face and took a few deep breaths.

Indirectly, I took several steps toward her...then a few more. In near silence, I had slipped to just a dozen feet away from her.

She did not move her feet; instead, her eyes rolled to look at me.

Immediately I looked at the ground. I did not want to frighten her or cause her to expend herself in any way. Like two watchmen guarding a post, we both stood fast.

I glanced up to see that her eyes were so rolled in my direction that much of the white sclera surrounding her eye was visible. As her eye held mine, I rotated slightly so that she could only see one of my eyes. For most horses, to be engaged with both eyes of another being is considered stalking, while to be watched with only one eye is merely observing. I continued to watch.

Her white-rimmed eye held mine.

There, like a distant beacon winking within the frigid, drab light, I could see it...an ember within her was still burning. Although her body was very near death...her will was not. She was still fighting. As horrific as she appeared, she had not yet given up hope...and neither would I.

Troy's hand gently squeezed my shoulder as he joined me and whispered into my ear, "She's the one. Of all these horses, she is the 'least of the least'...the one that needs help the most. Truly, she is why we are here...when she is able, she is the one that will come home with us."

In silence we stood hand in hand, quietly verifying the new pact between us. A thinness in the low cloud cover allowed weak yellow shafts of sunlight to filter through. Hope was beginning to flow.

After what seemed to many of us as some of the longest hours of our lives, two final locations were found for the horses. It was around one o'clock when the good news arrived. The lieutenant in charge gathered the volunteers together and made the long awaited announcement. The first location was in Bend, about twenty-five miles away and in close proximity to a veterinary practice. This facility would be used to house the thirty horses that were the most critically ill. The second location would be the Deschutes County Fairgrounds in Redmond, which was about forty miles away. The livestock set-up which was already there would become the perfect place to house the remaining one hundred.

It was time for the long, dangerous process of moving the horses to begin.

The next daunting challenge was how to safely coax primarily unhandled horses into the claustrophobic confines of a horse trailer. As with most things in life that people are passionate about, everyone had their own distinct opinions of how they thought things should be accomplished. Although most of the officers and volunteers had skill in trailering horses, few had ever experienced the unique challenges associated with attempting to move truly wild horses.

Now that locations were determined and waiting to receive us, as a group we needed to start loading horses as quickly and safely as possible. Being unsure for so long as to even if we would be able to move the horses on this day, little had been organized in that direction.

Again, no equine rescue equaling this level of danger or volume had ever been attempted before. In the volunteers' efforts to help expedite the method of how to accomplish this monumental task, attitudes rose with tempers as the day wore on and no horses were yet loaded into the growing serpentine of waiting trailers. Everyone wanted what was best for the horses, which was ultimately to move them out of this living hell. In an effort to make this happen, the lieutenant and officers were being verbally pulled into pieces by strong personalities that fought to be heard.

Shortly after the announcement had been made, one volunteer took it upon himself to try and load a stallion with hooves so horrifically overgrown that they curled upward and backward toward his knees like grotesque "slippers." Although frightened, the stallion was readily trying to step up into the trailer. Yet every time the horse lifted his leg, his hoof would catch and bang on the underside of the trailer bumper. Many watched in rising hopelessness as the weakening stallion tried over and over to accomplish such a seemingly simple task. As the stallion's strength ebbed, his sense of discouragement flowed, until in utter exhaustion he gave up completely. Everything about the body language of this fatigued horse indicated that he sadly believed that what was being asked of him was impossible.

Unfortunately, perhaps acknowledging that daylight was fleeting by, the volunteer lost his temper and began to lash the spent horse until the horse collapsed in absolute exhaustion under the trailer. Among those who came to give aid, this incident incited a verbal riot. Everyone was so anxious to help, yet no one seemed to know how or where to start.

Several women literally ran up to Troy and begged him to do *something*. Before he could answer, their composure disintegrated like an earthen dam besieged by a flood. Their frustration, anger, and anxiety gushed out in a wash of tearful words pleading for a "kinder" solution.

Understandably, the emotional intensity of the day was exacting a toll on everyone. There were so many more people with far greater horse experience there than Troy and I; who were we to go to the front and lead others with vastly superior skills? It was already after one o'clock, and our window of daylight would soon be closing.

Very quietly, Troy asked the lieutenant if he could please try to move a few of the stallions off the little hillside up by the garbage pile. While talking on one cell phone and waiting for a reply on another, the overwhelmed lieutenant simply nodded and waved Troy in the direction of the trash heap. That was good enough for us.

In our earlier evaluation, we had noticed that many of the stallions that were being kept in the pens had, in fact, been handled before. We were able to approach several who allowed us to scratch them a bit. These would be the first few that we would try to convince that a better life lay waiting for them on the other end of this trailer ride.

I went to our truck and retrieved all of the rope halters that we had brought with us. Troy expertly backed our three-horse trailer through a maze of downed fences, tiny pens, and trash. When he was as close to the corral of amiable stallions as he could safely maneuver, he shut off the ignition and met me behind the trailer. There, in the fading light of the afternoon, we held hands and prayed. Both of us asked for wisdom, for ourselves and everyone else present…wisdom to do something we had never done or seen before…load 130 wild horses.

The first pen held two adult stallions that had obviously been living together for quite some time. Both allowed us to quietly approach and catch them with ease. With gentle reassurance, Troy let the first stallion know that he meant him no harm and that all would be well. The first stud stepped right up into the trailer without hesitation.

The second stallion was a monstrous paint that stood easily more than sixteen hands. Had he been inclined to do so, he could have seriously hurt anyone who got close enough. Instead, he was a perfect gentleman and, like the first stallion, peacefully stepped up into the trailer.

The third stallion was living alone in a tangled wire pen that shared a common line with the pen of the two horses already in the trailer. He was a very small, very beautiful black and white colt. By the time Troy and I had convinced him to come and just "look" at the trailer...a small crowd had started to form.

This stallion was clearly the youngest, and perhaps had never been in a trailer before. As Troy led him up to the open door, he balked and snorted in fear. Although most who had gathered were there in hopeful support, some of the "strong personalities" voiced jeers that rose like fiery arrows flying toward our backs. "You can't load stallions side by side, they'll kill each other!" and "He's never been in a trailer...whatta ya think you're gonna do? Just walk him right in?" and "That big paint horse is gonna kick the fire outta that little black and white guy!"

Troy stood with a very "soft" posture and just stroked the youngster's neck. I could tell that he was praying. More onlookers were arriving by the minute. Everyone was there to help...but truly no one knew how to start. In my heart, I joined Troy in praying that this frightened young horse would trust him enough to "step up" with him.

Very gently, Troy began to ask the young horse to move forward toward the waiting box. To everyone's great surprise, the colt lifted his left front foot...but not quite high enough. His effort was rewarded with nothing more than banging his hoof against the rubber bumper of the trailer. Several times the youngster repeated this process with the same result. He was lifting his foot up…just not high enough to reach the trailer floor.

I knew what Troy was thinking. If he could just "show" the young horse how high to lift his foot, the colt would probably do the rest himself. In what is certainly a very dangerous maneuver, Troy began to run his hand down the back of the colt's front leg. As the horse picked his foot up in response to the gentle pressure Troy applied…Troy moved his foot to the trailer floor.

In silence, Troy turned and just looked at me. I knew exactly what he was asking me to do. While gently raising my arms, I took several very measured steps toward the young stallion's rump. He glanced at my approach and began to slightly cower in the hind end.

Troy hinted for him to come forward. The attentive colt slowly lifted up his other front foot. Now, both his front feet were inside the trailer.

Together, we paused to allow the youngster time to process this new accomplishment. While speaking only to the horse, Troy softly rubbed his neck and shoulder. After several moments, Troy glanced at me again; it was time. Again, I silently raised my arms and stepped toward the horse. Like a little Cub Scout going on his first outing, with ears up he hopped right into the trailer. I quickly closed the door in case he changed his mind. He didn't. He seemed completely content to be in the space he was in. I let Troy slip out the back and secured the door for travel.

Upon noticing his new "bunkmate," the giant stallion in the middle of the trailer announced that he would be the boss by bellowing with earsplitting volume. "That's your cue!" I yelled to Troy, who was already in the truck cab preparing to leave. By putting the truck in its lowest gear and allowing it to literally inch forward, he shifted the concentration of all three of the stallions to their feet and staying balanced, instead of who would be king. While barely rolling forward, the trio of horses began to trailer like peaceful, four-legged peas in a pod.

The results of this tiny victory garnered an unexpected response. I watched in private awe as visible tension surrendered into visible relief. Many individuals were absently nodding in agreement as the full trailer pulled away. A few women even shared a high five, muffled by gloved hands. This is what we had all come for; this simple action was our uniting cause.

Troy, with a cowboy's nod and a thumb's up to me, was the first to leave this nightmarish site with a full trailer of "evacuees." While waving back at my sweet man, I couldn't help but feel deeply moved by his silent kindness and leadership. Choosing to stay behind, I would follow the fresh path that he had cleared and help organize the mass relocation that was to quickly follow.

The collective sparks of hope bolstered by this minor success ignited into an unstoppable flame. The door had been opened, now it was time to move forward, shoulder to shoulder. The volunteers began to lay aside their own "agendas" and come together as a team...a team that had a *big job* to do.

In that moment, I couldn't help but realize that there are times in this life when it is not the most educated or skilled who are ultimately equipped to lead...sometimes it is the one who just simply steps forward. It is not enough to merely know what is right...we must *do* what is right.

Everything changes when we shift our perspective to God's. His focus is on our mustard seed of faith...not our mountain of doubt. He realizes all that we are…not all that we are not. He sees all that we have…not all that we lack. God desires only what I have…and He does only what I cannot.

When we view our problems from the same perspective… anything can be possible. Anything *becomes* possible when we choose to lay our fear aside and simply…step up.

*Young Wisdom*

John, age 14, when asked which class in school he enjoyed the most: "Ummmm…*lunch!*"

Jenna, age 6, when speaking about how much Lightfoot loves her: "I don't mind his scars; I just see how much he loves me.

# 9

# Phoenix

After what had already been an extreme and emotionally charged day, it was time to go to work. The Sheriff's Department had been made aware of the miserable plight of 130 horses in need, and with great difficulty was finally able to secure two safe locations where they could be moved.

My gaze lingered on the back of our truck and trailer as Troy slowly pulled away from the rescue sight with the first three rescued horses. With a tiny twinge of sadness, I knew that he would not be returning. We both acknowledged that it would probably be best if he stayed at the Fairgrounds, one of the two locations that had been selected to house the needy horses, where he could help with the "receiving process" as the equine refugees arrived.

I had been quietly requested to stay behind and help organize the ensuing exodus. Since few of the horses had ever been touched by a human being, the task at hand was going to be a very complicated and dangerous one.

Apparently after hearing how Troy had been able to trailer the first three stallions, the incident commander had officially given me the go-ahead to assemble a working crew and begin loading horses.

It was now nearly two o'clock, and with the official "green light" to proceed, we were able to formulate how we were going to move wild horses into trailers with whatever "tools" we could find around the decaying ranch. Together with many friends, we hastily constructed a "catch pen," chute, and collapsible loading pen out of all of the semi-usable metal panels that we could find on the property.

Because most of these horses had never been handled, attempting to halter them was completely out of the question. We would begin by pushing approximately a dozen horses at a time into the catch pen. Here, each horse needed to first be processed and documented as evidence for the Sheriff's Department before it could be loaded into one of the dozens of waiting trailers. This was a very tedious process that took great concentration from many of the volunteers. Within the milling herd in the catch pen, every horse had to be photographed, assigned a general description, and identified by breed, gender, age, weight, and condition. (It was agreed that the three horses Troy had already moved would be processed as soon as they reached their new location.)

Once the "scribes" who were in charge of recording all the gathered information were in place and ready, the rest of the group quietly moved out into the main herd. This group of horses was for all practical purposes "loose." The area through which they roamed was so great that the only fence line in view was the one that ran next to the dwelling and other deterio- rated corrals. Thankfully, it was to our advantage that loose hay had been put out for this herd very close to the area where we would be trying to move them into the catch pen.

With great caution, thirty or so of the volunteers made a "human fence" through the milling mob. As gently as we could, our line began to slowly push a small group of horses toward the catch pen. Our goal was to keep the entire group of horses as calm as possible. With civilians on the ground moving through a herd of wild horses, we didn't want the horses to be frightened and run, or worse, run us over.

We had baited them with piles of fresh hay like bread crumbs into the waiting catch pen. Lured by their overwhelming hunger, many of the younger horses walked right into the scenario we had planned. Some of the older mares, being more savvy, cagey, and experienced, knew that we intended to do more than just feed them. As we continued to walk shoulder to shoulder and an arm's length apart, some of the wiser mares began to circle, looking for a way of escape. Immediately we stopped, giving the horses with rising concern time to settle. With heads held high, they watched our every move through extremely suspicious eyes.

It became eminently clear that no settling was going to happen here; these feral mares believed that something very bad was coming their way. In nearly instantaneous unison, they wheeled and broke into a gallop straight for the human line! By waving our arms we averted several in the stampede, but one large gray mare would not be deterred. Her thundering posture left no question that she was going to break through whatever stood in her way.

Obviously not wishing for anyone to be trampled, we quickly made a gap for her to safely pass through. As my friend Vicky moved to the side, she looked up just in time to see that the eye of the charging mare nearest to her was white—the mare was partially blind! Vicky lunged to the left in a not so fluid move that probably would have cost any cat most if not all of its nine lives! The rushing mare brushed Vicky with the outside of her shoulder and forcefully spun her to the ground. Being completely nonplussed, Vicky just sat on the cold earth and began to laugh. "I saw that blind eye coming at me and just thought, 'Girl, today just isn't your day!'" Everyone joined her hearty laughter—certainly not because it was funny, but with great relief that she was truly okay.

Daylight was beginning to weaken as we finally were able to find a rhythm. Trucks pulling their trailers formed an organized line that looked more like a collective multicolored locomotive than individuals offering whatever rig they had to help move the refugees. One team was responsible for moving horses into the catch pen. Another was accountable for all the "cleric work" of documenting each horse. Still another team was in charge of determining how many horses could be herded into each trailer, and then safely executing this without getting charged, kicked, or trampled in the process.

Since the horses were too wild to handle individually, we had to "free" load them. This meant that no stall doors or dividers could be used to ensure the horses' safe travels within the trailer once it started to move. To counter-balance this lack of physical device to help steady the horses, we chose instead to let the horses hold each other up. This meant that instead of loading three horses in a three-horse trailer with dividers…we would tie the dividers to the side of the trailer and would free-load five horses…or even six, if they were small.

Once we determined how many horses could safely fit into each trailer, my team would herd them into the collapsible "loading pen." With the trailer door fully open, we would "convince" the horses that the very best place for them to be was inside the box before them. We accomplished this by using "flags," usually a plastic bag tied on the end of a stick. When waved, the whisked, plastic sound was unfamiliar to the horses and would cause them to move away from the strange source of noise. This "system" was very effective in turning the horses to face the waiting trailer. Once most of them were turned, we would collapse the pen to gently "push" them in.

After approximately two hours of loading one pen after another of starving, terrified horses, the next group that filed past me contained the skeletal filly. She was the most gruesomely starved creature I had ever seen. Troy and I had agreed earlier that if she miraculously lived through this ordeal, when she was released from the impending investigation, we would take her home.

In her severely weakened condition, Troy and I had noted before that any movement was hard for her. Yet, when adrenalized by fear, she moved along at a brisk and very stiff-legged walk. She was the smallest in a group of five others who were to be loaded next.

Once the tiny herd entered our collapsible pen, we closed the makeshift gate behind them. Immediately feeling trapped, like all the other groups, they began to quickly circle, collectively looking for a way of escape. As gently as we could, we turned the group to face the opening that led into the waiting trailer. With great caution, we began to "ask" the horses to move forward into the trailer by making the pen smaller behind them. Frightened by the pressure from behind, two of the horses lunged forward.

Suddenly, but not entirely unexpectedly, the entire group circled hard to the left in an effort to avoid the unfamiliar box in front of them. The emaciated filly was abruptly pushed sideways in front of the trailer opening. Before we could stop them, the stronger horses spun around again. Swiftly realizing the trailer was their best way of escape, they began driving hard against the suddenly trapped, sideways filly. In an instant, this extremely fragile filly's legs were being crushed against the bumper of the trailer! Perhaps expecting that she was about to see all four spindly legs break, the woman holding back the trailer door screamed!

Instantly, two of our team lunged to reach their flags in front of the driving horse's faces and stop their forward momentum. Everyone seemed to hold their breath as the weak filly slowly was able to regain her balance and turn toward the trailer.

With everyone turned in the correct direction, all the flags were lowered. Ever so gently, again, we asked the little herd to move forward. In near unison, all five safely jumped into the trailer. Once the door was secured, we checked through the windows to make sure that all, especially the filly, were in a firmly supported position to make the trip to the intensive care facility.

Mercifully, as the afternoon wore on, no horses or people were injured during the loading process. We continued to evaluate each horse-to-trailer ratio—seven horses in this large trailer, twelve horses in that even bigger one, five in the next. The caravan of trucks pulling trailers continued to slowly rotate forward until it became too dark to safely continue.

Fatigue and relief spread over the volunteers in union with the gathering darkness. In a handful of hours the combined teams of volunteers had safely moved just under one hundred horses. That alone was a decent accomplishment with tame horses…yet, these were wild horses, individuals who had rarely, if ever, been touched.

The remaining horses were moved the following day. The exodus to safety was complete.

After a few days had passed for the horses to settle and rest, it was time to begin their extensive vetting process. Dozens of horses had hooves that were so long that they had difficulty moving correctly, and many of these suffered severe soft-tissue and tendon damage as well. We knew, because of their time frame at their desert purgatory, that no horse under the age of five had ever been vaccinated or dewormed or had hoof care of any kind. After moving all the horses only days before, we were also convinced that every horse under the age of five had known virtually no human contact. This vetting process was not only daunting by the sheer volume of horses, it was going to be *extremely* dangerous as well.

Troy and I arrived early at the fairgrounds with several of our staff. Weak rays of sunlight were no match for the bitter gray chill of the December morning. Together we joined cold hands behind our truck and prayed for safety over what was to be laid before us. All of us fully understood the risk involved, how completely treacherous every aspect of what needed to be done on this day would be. *Lord, protect us all.*

When we joined the rest of the volunteers and deputies, the lieutenant who was the incident commander rallied the hardy team for instruction. There were veterinarians, vet technicians, farriers, horse trainers, first-aid responders, horse wranglers, and dozens of others with varied horse experience just like us. Immediately, we were heavily cautioned that this job was going to be so dangerous that it had already been arranged where the Air-Life helicopter would land if our safety precautions failed.

Because we were at the fairgrounds, we intended to make full usage of the labyrinth of holding pens, bucking chutes, and movable metal panels, plus the main arena. Our objective was to further document and administer as much care as we could. Each and every horse would first be haltered and then thoroughly recorded with multiple photographs. Then they were numbered, assigned an estimated age through dentition, injected with a vaccine that protects against five major equine diseases, given a dose of nasal spray that combats an extremely virulent virus called "strangles," and also administered an oral dose of dewormer. Next, the veterinarians would deal with any wounds that needed professional attention. And finally, each horse's hooves would be evaluated and trimmed, if absolutely necessary, by some incredibly brave farriers.

In conclusion, the entire herd would be sorted. Adult stallions would be placed in individual pens, adult mares—who were nearly all in foal—would be corralled together. All the young colts would all be placed in a separate corral together and all the fillies would be gathered into a separate corral.

For helping a wild horse that had known little or no human contact, attempting all this was truly expecting nearly the impossible. For *one hundred* wild horses with little or no human contact, it would become nothing less than a miracle. It was our prayer that we would be able to accomplish this for every terrified horse without any injuries…or anyone being killed!

After a bit of shuffling, the volunteers were organized into basic teams. The mounted horse wranglers would move the different groups of horses into a common pen where they could drive them into a long "hallway." As every horse progressed down the "hall," the different teams would perform their specific tasks. Eventually, each horse would end up in one of the three bucking chutes where one of three medical teams would administer their restorative care.

Although the entire process was fraught with danger, confining a wild horse in a three-by-ten-foot metal space was, at times, nearly suicidal.

Horses are herd animals first and range animals second. This means that they need each other and they need space to feel safe. It broke my heart that we had to deny them both of those things, temporarily, in order to prepare each individual for the new life that awaited them. Once in the bucking chute, they were so utterly terrified that they were reduced to nothing more than pure survival instincts. Nearly all of them entered the chute and immediately dropped their head to the ground in a frenzied panic, desperately searching for a way of escape. Their entire bodies trembled and shook at the sheer thought of being touched.

As one of the leaders for the vetting teams, I always tried to calm each horse before working on it by slowly rubbing its withers the same way a mother would nurture her foal. For many this worked well; for others it had the same effect as pushing the "eject button" in a fighter jet! Consumed with white-hot terror, these horses would literally launch straight up in a frenzy of flailing hooves. As much as it saddened me to be part of the cause of their alarm, I *had* to touch them to get the job done. I didn't fully realize until that day that horses, when motivated, really *can* climb metal!

We quickly learned the benefits of looping cotton ropes over their backs and securing them to the metal panels. This way the horses were not only prevented from rearing straight up, they were also effectively stopped from climbing the panels. This was a great relief to all of us, because during their crashing panic, several horses had already gotten their hooves and legs *through* the panels—which, without a quick resolution... could have been fatal.

The farriers were amazing. To volunteer for such incredibly dangerous work gave me even more respect for these individuals who I already highly honor. Numerous times throughout the day I saw teams of as many as four grown men trying to steady a single youngster while one man attempted to trim its hooves. Even though they employed every precaution they could to be as safe as possible, several times throughout the day I saw the entire team get taken out and dragged through the freezing slush. Once during the afternoon I turned around just in time to see one farrier receive a double-barreled kick square in the chest from a wily colt. In typical cowboy fashion, he steadied himself with a few backwards steps, turned the air blue, and got right back to business.

Certainly the horses with the worst feet were the adult stallions. These poor souls had been confined to tiny pens and subjected to stand in their own manure for the last four years. Some of them had hooves that were so long and curled backwards that the only safe remedy was to tranquilize them until they were flat on the ground, and then saw the sickening "slippers" off with a hacksaw.

Freezing rain turned to sloppy snow and then rain again. Despite the miserable weather, everyone worked together like links in a supportive chain. Each individual deputy, horse professional, and volunteer all joined arms with those beside them and gave what they had. Slowly, horse by individual horse, hand by individual hand, the impossible job was finally completed.

In the face of many bumps, bruises, kicks, and countless "near misses," the Air-Life helicopter never landed nor was any ambulance ever dispatched. No serious injury was sustained by either man or beast. At the day's end, even those who wouldn't claim to be "religious" were caught giving a smile and a "thumb's up" toward the heavens.

As word of the horses' rescue spread, the monetary impact of the recovery effort was immediately realized. The financial resources needed to sustain 130 seriously neglected and starved horses was staggering. The necessary feed, hay, medical attention, medical supplies, and rent for the fairgrounds and intensive care facility quickly made the Millican Horse Rescue national news.

Truly, what an amazing nation we live in. With so many other worthy causes all asking for support, who would care to give aid to 130 unwanted horses? To our great relief, *many* cared. As the cry for help traveled across this great land…the answer in return was a firm and resounding "Yes, we will help." Scores of generous hearts not only took heed…they acted… giving whatever extra financial help they could afford.

As monetary help started to pour in, the Animal Control Department of the Deschutes County Sheriff's Office and dozens of volunteers set about focusing on this desperate herd and what their long-term care was going to be.

Besides the one hundred horses being housed at the fairgrounds, there were thirty more horses in an intensive care facility that needed exhaustive attention. Close to a dozen were half or completely blind. The very worst of the lame and emaciated horses were there as well…including the little skeletal creature that had earlier stolen both Troy's and my heart.

My first visit to the intensive care facility came only days after the exodus was completed. Following the directions that had been sketched on a crumpled piece of paper, I turned onto a narrow, twisting, paved driveway. As my simple notes indicated,

I drove past a small veterinary practice and continued a short distance to what looked like a private home. Just west of the home was what looked to be the makeshift ICU ward.

The building was shaped in a basic *T* pattern. A dozen or more stalls made up what would be the top of the letter, and the "stem" was a large, covered arena. It was late in the day, and the barn appeared empty of people. I walked down the main corridor, gleaning information with every step. The stalls were filled with the most desperate horses. Each door had been labeled with feeding instructions, a medication schedule, and a "barn name" for identification.

While walking down the corridor, I looked through the barred windows at each huddled soul. Stall after stall seemed to enclose a new variation of acute equine suffering. One held a partially blind stallion who was severely lame; in another a young stallion with a serious wound to his shoulder; still another held a completely blind mare who had learned to depend on her adult son to guide her…both had hooves that had grown into gruesome curling abnormalities and were now so incredibly lame that they could barely walk. Even though they were safe, fed, and dry, my broken thoughts kept stumbling over the same stone: How could someone allow this to happen, for so long…to so many?

The next information board read "Jack and Jill." Here she was…the emaciated filly that I had truly come to see. Of the starving horses, she was the very worst. In an attempt to lower her stress, she was placed in an indoor stall with a small outdoor run. She was also assigned a roommate whose condition was nearly as bad as hers. He was estimated to be a one-and-a-half-year-old colt, predominantly of quarter horse heritage. Like the filly, he was also a dull bay color with high white socks on both his hind legs…which only accentuated how incredibly long those legs were for his destitute body. He looked more like an awkward carnival attraction on stilts than a young horse.

Wednesdays became my appointed day to clean all the stalls and replenish the feed and water levels for every resident. Often notes were written on a dry erase board with special instructions for more needy individuals. Once all the "chores" were completed, I always spent extra quiet time bonding with "my girl." Everyone involved with the horse rescue effort was well aware that this little misbegotten pariah had stolen my heart, like the last unwanted puppy in the pound.

She, like most of the others, had never been handled except to administer various medications, which included many vaccinations and deworming paste. Since most of this was usually completed earlier in the week, I wanted to make sure that while I was there, she would be handled by someone who was simply there to love her. At the end of each day, together we would practice a small amount of being haltered and led, and picking up our feet. This was rewarded with a special mix of grain and extremely gentle grooming.

News of my devotion to this little urchin traveled to the top of the tree. Lieutenant Mark, who was in charge, had become a close friend through this experience, and he pulled me aside one day and simply said, "If it were up to me alone, I would just give her to you today. You have certainly earned the right to have her. Yet because this is an ongoing investigation, we must follow procedure. We have to see this through to the very end…by the book." For someone in such a high position of authority, it was always clear that Mark's compassion for these horses was never far from the surface. He, as with the rest of the volunteer "family," had grown to love, respect, and occasionally dread the individuals of this ragged herd that we had become so vested in.

Without a doubt, my favorite filly was one of the most homely horses that I had ever seen. Instead of looking like a starving young horse, the rampant lanugo that covered her body made her look more like a bizarre, wooly apparition. Her nappy coat, which was completely ineffective in keeping the skin on her back from freezing off, apparently was remarkably efficient in trapping a horrific odor that seemed to cling to her like a sickening plague. The little girl just *stunk!* Once home, like clockwork, I could be found every Wednesday afternoon stripping down in my tiny laundry room and putting my "contaminated" clothing directly into the washer. Sadly, my hands and fingernails were a different matter. No amount of perfumed soap could go "toe to toe" with the rotting flesh stench that clung to them after visiting my stinky girl.

Nevertheless, I loved this little filly, and it would take more than the smell of death to keep me away from her side.

Because her physical condition was so dire, changes in her weight were not immediately discernable. It was the small changes in her attitude that continued to rise like a brilliant fireweed through the ashes of her former life. After many weeks of balanced "recovery feeding," on one of my Wednesday visits, as I had done nearly every Wednesday before, I released my special girl into the arena for some self-appointed exercise. Unexpectedly, she took several trotting steps and then threw in a couple of feeble attempts at bucking! She felt good enough to try and play! I was so excited that I joined in with some "whoops and wahoos" of encouragement. This seemed to be the fuel she needed. Instead of slowing down, she broke into a very awkward canter, punctuated by all sorts of goofy attempts to throw her heels up. I couldn't help but laugh out loud at her faltering display of joyful rejuvenation.

———— ||| ————

For the following three months, many of my staff and I could be found balancing our volunteer efforts between "vetting weekends" at the fairgrounds and cleaning, vetting, and "gentling" the infirmed horses at the intensive care facility. Helping to care for this herd of horses had truly become a part of our weekly routine.

The Sheriff's Department had been able to finalize a plan to auction off the rescued horses on March 3 to "approved buyers only." This meant that everyone who wished to purchase a rescued horse had to fill out some very detailed paperwork and pass a criminal background check. The purpose of the "check" was to attempt to prevent any of these horses from ever falling through the cracks again. Potential buyers were also required to sign an agreement that the horses they purchased were to be kept for at least one year. Upon the completion of that first year, they could resell the horses to a suitable home if they so chose.

With this decision firmly in place came great relief...and anxiety. The Sheriff's Department and volunteers were thrilled that these refugees would finally have a real, nurturing home. Yet we began to hear fragments of information that some of those who wished to purchase a "rescued" horse had never owned a horse before...and a few were hoping to buy these horses for their children! Apparently, to a handful of recently approved buyers, there just didn't seem to be a clear understanding that most of these horses were still *wild*. Of the one hundred or so who were recovering at the fairgrounds, only a couple could actually be approached and touched.

This alarming information spurred many of the volunteers to start working in earnest with all the intensive care horses, to help them simply become halter broke. To our relief, a few of the older horses in the facility gradually remembered the training of their youth. Sadly, as we already knew, the remaining horses under the age of five had never been handled before this ordeal and truly did not wish to begin now.

Armed with nothing more than intense compassion and a steely nerve, my friend Kris began entering the stalls of some of the most terrified…and dangerous individuals. To step inside a sealed, twelve-by-twelve-foot space with a wild animal that is many times your size is extremely hazardous to say the least. Yet sending these frightened animals out into the real world without giving them the tools to safely deal with a new environment…could be disastrous. It would not be unlike sending a soldier on a mission without any training. Clearly, it was not a scenario lending itself toward safety or success for either horse or new owner.

All the volunteers understood the perilous ramifications of auctioning off wild horses. Yet Kris, more than any other person, took action toward equipping the most dangerous of these refugees. Many a morning she could be found in the most risky stalls of the intensive care facility. While taking every precaution necessary to ensure her safety, her mission was simple: "round pen" the wildest individuals within their twelve-foot stall, until they turned to face her. Once the horse rotated toward her, she would begin building trust by gently touching the muzzle, cheek, and forehead. She consistently repeated this process until she could touch the entire horse without a violent reaction. As she piloted the way, other volunteers followed until the fears of all the critical-care horses were eased enough so that they could be safely haltered and led.

---

It was March 2, the day before the Millican Horse Rescue Auction. After months of rehabilitative care, our extended family of horses would soon be leaving us, purchased into their new life.

As part of a caravan that was moving all the ICU horses to the fairgrounds, I drove my truck and trailer filled with three young horses. As I followed others before me to the gated main entry behind the barns, a uniformed officer stopped me. Like those before me, he requested my driver's license to check against a list of those who had clearance to enter. I watched as he tapped it absently against the clipboard that he was searching to find my name. Looking up with a smile, he announced, "You're good to go, Mrs. Meeder."

I pulled up into a line of trucks and trailers whose drivers were waiting their turn. All were needed to swing their rigs around and back them up an enormous distance to snug their full trailers directly against the corrals where the horses they carried would spend the night. While waiting, my emotions teetered as if on a high wire, balancing atop all my dichotomous feelings. My head acknowledged that being adopted tomorrow would probably make for one of the best days of their lives. Yet my intuition continued to cry out like a herald, warning of one improbable and negative outcome after another.

Although cleared, what happens if these "buyers" do not have the best of intentions for these horses? This is exactly how the offending couple was able to start what became this present suffering herd. What happens if the buyers are well-intended but inexperienced with wild horses? A year from now, they could sell their horses to someone who appears nice, but who could ultimately turn around and sell them to a meat buyer if they chose to. What happens if these horses are placed in proximity with someone's children? The children could be unintentionally hurt or even killed by these wary, frightened animals who, apart from most of the ICU horses, are still too wild to handle. *Lord, let Your wisdom fall...* I prayed while rubbing my brow.

It was now my turn to back up my trailer the crazy distance that separated the line of trucks from the temporary corrals. With all the eyes of the Sheriff's Department and volunteers watching, I was suddenly grateful that years of living on a tiny ranch had served me well through the necessity of being able to back up anything, anywhere.

Once my horses were settled into their respective corrals, I parked my truck and sought out my special filly. Although I had pushed it down for months, the very real possibility surfaced within me that this could very well be my last day with her. Other buyers were coming who had far more financial power than I. It was possible that the resources I had to purchase this filly...would not be enough.

Understanding the situation from afar, some very dear friends of mine sent financial help all the way from their home in England with the intention of facilitating her purchase. In deepest appreciation of their thoughtful gift, I asked them if they would choose the honor—if it worked out that she would become ours—to name this humble little soul. They responded by sending me several potential name choices. One of their name possibilities instantly rose above all the others. In silence, I hid it within my heart.

All of the preparations for the auction had been completed. Every horse had been moved into the appropriate corral and fitted with a nylon collar that held their bidding number. Every form was filled out, every security measure was in place, all was ready for the horses to be released into a new season. Even though I had helped with many of these tasks and *knew* these things to be true…fear continued to swamp my heart.

Of all my watery "what ifs," my deepest pool of doubt contained only one question: "What if someone else buys my girl?" Even with the added gift from my friends, the outcome of this auction was wide open. Not being a woman of great financial means…it was certainly possible.

Hundreds of people were coming from all over the Northwest to buy these horses. The parking area at the fairgrounds was already beginning to fill with trucks pulling large…expensive…horse trailers. Truly, this was the point, the purpose of why so many of us worked so hard to get these refugees prepared for a better life, a new hope. This is what I wanted for *all* the horses…all but one.

My heart warped with the painful realization that my precious little horse, the least of the least that had survived so much, might not come home with me. Today might possibly be the last day that I would know her, and know she was safe…and that every stinking hair on her homely body was thoroughly and completely loved.

*Lord, probably every person who steps up into the stadium with a bidding card tomorrow will have more in their pocket than I have. Any one of them could outbid me for my beloved filly. I love her so much, Lord…help me to rest in Your will, knowing that You will choose what is truly best for her. You have proven throughout my entire life that You are faithful…that You are worthy to be trusted.*

*No matter what happens, if she goes home in my trailer or someone else's...I trust You, Lord...because I know that You love her more.*

After I had spent as much time as I could with my little girl in this new corral, and had given her all the compassion I had...it was time for me to leave her side. *Surround her, Lord, with all your protection, grace, and love*, I prayed. I secured her gate behind me and quietly walked away. I clearly understood that this might very well be our last moment together.

———————‖———————

Early the next morning, rays of sunlight shattered the early gray skies with brilliant, golden spears rising like arrows from the frozen horizon. Today was the day. I was completely brimming with anticipation and fulfillment for all that was to come.

Together, the volunteers had worked hard for months to bring these horses back from the brink of destruction. Today would be the satisfying conclusion of all our combined efforts. I was settled, and my heart was full of peace.

I walked down the hill from our home into the main yard of the ranch and met many of my faithful and warmly dressed staff. We circled together, joining gloved hands, and prayed as a team for the well-being and correct placement of every horse. Frozen breath rose from our circle like the welcome, steaming aroma of our prayers rising toward the Lord. I couldn't help but imagine, as I often do: Were God's hands around us...cradling us close to His face...just as we hold a steaming drink on a freezing day? It's an image that always makes me smile.

It was time. We all loaded up into the ranch truck and carefully pulled down the hill. Our spirits soaring, wide-open hope was as apparent and easy to see as the symbol that we pulled behind us…our empty horse trailer.

———— ||| ————

The lively, metallic chatter of the auctioneer was punctuated by the animated whoops and hollers of the spotters as they raised their clipboards high with every new bid that came from the full stadium. The main arena at the fairgrounds had been transformed with a maze of metal panels into what turned out to be a very efficient way of making each horse, when its turn to be purchased arrived, easy to view and available to the buyers. The enormous awning, which in the summer gave welcome shade for the seated spectators, on this day cast a broad-mantled shadow that was nearly too cold for many to endure. Most of the buyers and their families sat on coats, blankets, and even bidding cards to help insulate their backsides from the bone-chilling cold of the shiny metal bleachers. But even as cold as it was, any discomfort it might have brought was no match for the bright mood of this day.

Every volunteer was in place, assisting in some specific way to help smooth out the flow of the event. In truth, little could have kept us away from helping our extended family of horses make the transition into their new homes.

The mature stallions were auctioned off first, followed by the adult mares. To the joy of those in the stadium, two mares had already successfully delivered their foals. To the relief of the volunteers, all were healthy. I knew that the young fillies would be next, followed by the colts. The last corrals of horses to be auctioned off would be those who were transported from the intensive care facility. Their makeshift corrals were located far to the right of the stadium. Later, this would mean that any-one who wished to bid on them would have to leave their seat and walk down to the simple maze of corrals to get a better look at these "special need" horses.

I would have to wait to the very end of the day…to know my answer.

All the volunteers were briefed as to how the auction would flow. We knew that the bidding would start at what would be considered fair-market value for each individual. If no one bid on the horse, it would be returned to its former corral, and after the main auction was finished, a "half price" auction would be instated to help sell the "less sellable" horses.

After many hours and many horses being processed through the main arena, it was clear that approximately seven out of ten horses were finding a home their first time in the ring.

The auction was winding down. It was nearly time for the "ICU" horses to be sold. Because these were blind, or severely lame, or ruthlessly starved, they were to be auctioned off directly from their private corrals that had been constructed the day before. Even though all these horses were improved, for some the stress of walking too far was more strain than we wished to enforce on them. At this stage in their recovery, it was easier to have the potential buyers walk the short distance down to them.

The auctioneer announced that those with a special benev-olence for the ICU horses would need to leave the stadium and file down toward the horses' corrals. I was amazed and deeply pleased to see how many individuals came down and gathered around "the hospital" in hopes of purchasing the most needy horses of the event.

I left my post-position as a volunteer…to become a bidder.

After climbing up and finding a seat on top of a confluence of metal panels, I was better able to look over the crowd and see which horse was being auctioned. Because these horses could not be individually presented to the group, the group was required to crowd around each pen as they were being auctioned off.

As fate would have it, the auctioneer started at the far end of the makeshift ICU ward. That meant that "my" horse would be sold next to last.

The auction staggered on with the brutal lethargy of a slug going up hill. I am certain that I could actually see my own hair growing longer! Waiting for the moment of revelation—would I have more days to love this little waif, or not?—was by now a painful process. Would I drive away from this place with an empty trailer...or one filled with the skinniest, furriest, stinkiest, most lovable little horse I had ever seen?

"Number 567...number 567...a bay filly is next!" The auctioneer's words jolted through my chest like electricity...

*This is it*, I thought to myself. The auctioneer began: "The bidding will start at...at...hmm. Well this little lady sure needs a home, so the bidding will start at one hundred dollars. Do I hear one-twenty-five? One-twenty-five? One-twenty-five?..."

Slightly huddled against the cold, she stood before them all wearing the most common color a horse can have. She looked more like a half-sheep, half-horse apparition than something anyone would want to buy. She was so unsightly, so pathetic, so unlovely...that the crowd was silent...*dead* silent. Not one person signaled a bid. The only sounds to be heard among the multitude came from folks quietly blowing into their cold hands and rubbing them together for warmth.

There she stood...within the midst of a large crowd...and

*not one* person wanted her. I couldn't help but wonder, "Of all these people, was there no one else?" I smiled broadly as I thought to myself, "I will be that one, I will be the *one* girl who loves the ugly, skinny, furry, stinky little horse."

Before I could raise my number, the auctioneer jerked to a new level of droning melodrama. *"One hundred twenty-five! Do I hear one-fifty? One-fifty? One-fifty?"* Immediately I noticed a man who had apparently been scratching his head and had accidentally been mistaken for casting a bid. He was desperately trying to get the auctioneer's attention and convince him it was all a mistake! He made it urgently clear to those around him that he did *not* want a horse that looked like her!

I *did* want her! Raising my numbered bidding card over my head, I waved it like a checkered flag at the end of a grueling race… for to me, that's exactly what it was. "One hundred fifty once…twice…*Sold!* For one hundred and fifty dollars to the happy woman on the fence!"

"God, You are so good!" I said, as I slipped down off the panels into the crowd. A man, hearing me and recognizing that I had just purchased the ugly horse in front of him, turned around and looked at me as if I had *two heads!* I smiled at him as I made my way through the crush toward *my* horse's corral. Prohibited from entering until the crowds moved away, I reached through the panels and ran my hand down as much of her neck as I could reach. Her head was not far from me. While looking into her eye nearest me, I realized that I hadn't dared until now to speak her name out loud…my precious "Phoenix" was coming home!

As I drove home, I couldn't help but let my thoughts and emotions soar. *Lord, this could have turned out so many different ways. Thank You for this…all of this.*

While contemplating all that had happened, it occurred to me that, just like our once unwanted and unloved property, trees, horses, and kids, so too this horse had come to us in a "superficial" state of disrepair. If she were truly revealed today as all that she would become tomorrow—just like our property, trees, horses, and kids—I would be completely unable to afford her; I would have no access into her life. It was precisely her "ugliness" that became the common key.

It was precisely *my* "ugliness phase," the season of time in my life when I was struggling to grow through the tragic loss of both my parents, that prepared my heart for all that was to come. I didn't realize it then, but that was the time when I was being "readied" to reach out to those around me who were struggling through their own "ugly phases."

Perhaps the most important thing to remember about an "ugly phase" within ourselves and those around us is that it's just that…a *phase*. It has a beginning and an end.

A phase can be much like the burned-up pine trees that Troy was once dispatched to take to the dump. Even though they had been through a fire and looked completely dead, when he scratched their bark...they were still green inside. While blackened and destroyed on the outside...they were still *alive* on the inside. Troy saw what they could become if given the opportunity to grow through their blackness. With time and care these same "throw-away" trees have grown through their charred past and grace our property with beauty to this day. I am so intensely grateful that in the times of my life when I was blackened and dead on the outside...the Lord did not cast me away; He knew that there was life within me still.

What an incredible honor and privilege it has been to follow the lead of my Lord and reach through the flames to pull out those who might temporarily be a little blackened and ugly on the outside, while knowing for a fact that there is life within them still. Just like me many years ago, what they needed most was a helping hand and someone to truly *see* them and believe in all that they *could* become.

It was the largest horse rescue in Oregon's history. And I was proud to be driving home with the most desperate, blackened, ugly horse of the entire herd. She was just like me...and I couldn't wait to see all that she was to become.

---

*Young Wisdom*

Cole, age 5, when trying to explain
how exciting riding is: "When I ride a horse,
it just makes my blood wiggle!"

# 10

## Love Matters

Love matters…perhaps more than we know. Pure love, refined of all the dross the world associates with it, changes our very foundations.

It is easy to become so caught up in how we think certain things should happen that we fail to realize that healing, release, forgiveness…"life" happens outside the little box of our understanding. Love can be like that.

Phoenix—whose name had been lovingly softened into a more feminine "Phoebe"—had finally come home. After her twilight-hour rescue and months in an intensive care facility, she was, at last, living on the ranch. Even after months of extensive nursing, she was still so shocking to look at that we prepared a special "recovery" paddock for her behind the main arena. This usually gave the staff and me a bit more time to verbally prepare our visitors for what they were about to see when meeting our newest charge.

The rampant lanugo that had once covered her body to conserve heat was now beginning to loosen its grip in the warmer days of spring. Handfuls of nearly three-inch-long wads of greasy hair were starting to fall off her body. Like an awkward puzzle, each newly revealed "piece" gave a tiny glimpse of the slender horse that was beginning to emerge.

Although she had been handled a great deal since her rescue, she was still in the process of becoming socialized with people. Much of Phoebe's early care was quite unpleasant for her, as it consisted of a myriad of vaccination and deworming cycles. Despite vetting discomforts, she was learning to trust. Daily it was becoming clearer to this little horse that regardless of her many unpleasant clinical procedures, people were generally kind and desired to give her much good will.

As Phoebe continued her quiet rehabilitation, the ranch staff and I started to see a very interesting pattern materialize. After her rescue from nearly fatal starvation and neglect, we wished to bring comfort, acceptance, relaxation, and general hygiene back to this orphan by simply spending time brushing her. Because brushing a horse is intrinsically a very nurturing act, on several occasions I encouraged women I knew—who had been through much abuse themselves—to just go and spend time brushing Phoebe.

There were many instances where I witnessed these same abused, battered, and neglected women come out of Phoebe's paddock in tears. When I asked them if everything was all right, to my surprise, they gave me remarkably similar answers: "I know that this just seems so silly…I really can't explain it…but when I am next to that little horse…just being with her…this small creature who has survived so much hardship… somehow she just seems to help me believe that I'm going to be all right too."

I knew exactly what these women were trying to communicate—because when I spent time with Phoebe, I felt the same way.

There was no denying it. Something about this simple little horse was changing many of those who spent time with her.

From its very humble beginning, the ranch has fervently

sought to serve those in need. Our ministry works hard to provide a unique place where the broken—broken of any kind—can find healing. Within our community, we shoulder with nearly every organization that deals with youth and family.

One group that we take great joy in serving is a local juvenile justice facility. Teenage boys work hard through a predetermined "levels" system to earn the right to come out to our ranch. For years, we have come to know them as being a truly spectacular group of young men. They are always polite, helpful, and willing to assist us with any task we lay before them. It has been my general observation that they are all really great guys who, for the most part, have had very weak parenting…especially from their fathers. For most, it appears that there has never been an upright, moral man in their lives to simply show them the way.

I *love* these guys…and they know it! It is such an inspiration to see them come to the ranch with a totally "clean slate" and watch them practice who they wish to become in the future. I rarely know anything about them or their background, so in my eyes, they get to rehearse being the perfect gentlemen.

Our day was just getting started when Sevi and Chloe, my two blue-heelers, announced that the boys had arrived slightly early. At the ranch, we do not wish to begin any day without first praying for every soul who might walk up our hill. I silently dismissed myself from the circle of bowed heads and gently closed the bunkhouse door behind me. I could see that there were about six young men walking with their counselor into the main yard of the ranch.

A few of the boys I knew well; some I did not know at all. Of the scattered details that I was aware of, it was my understanding that one of the boys coming today—I was told his name was Matt—would be here for his first time. He had been born to a mother who, perhaps during her pregnancy, loved drugs more than him. Her substance abuse had left him with a misshapened arm and hand. I was informed that he was an amazing young man who had grown up fighting with the world trying to prove that…he was not a *freak*.

As I walked down to meet the boys, I welcomed them with some goofy "Kim" greeting. Truly, I don't even know what I said; what I do know is that it is always my intention to make the boys feel "special" and at ease.

Introductions flowed easily between us. The boys stood in a loose circle, each acknowledging me in his own distinctive way. A few gave me a hug, some shook my hand, and a couple spoke their name and looked straight at the ground. As I continued to welcome the group, I was acutely aware of how much Matt did not want me to see his arm.

While acting completely oblivious to his "uniqueness" and treating him just like any other boy who comes to the ranch, I could feel my heart dropping like a very heavy anchor within my chest. I could not even begin to understand what his life must be like—the quick glances that snap back into long stares, the misguided questions, the torment from his weak-hearted peers.

This boy, who was hardly a boy in stature because he was already taller and heavier then I was, wanted me to see him for…him…not as the kid who was in any way different from any of the other guys in the circle.

His eyes told the story. They were a beautiful, clear blue that seemed to balance tenuously between acceptance and defiance. He very much wanted my approval and acceptance of him; otherwise he would have had no reason to hide his arm from me. Yet, if I were to disrespect him in any way, even a minimal way, I am certain that his defiance would rise up like a bitter shield of defense…once again attempting to deflect the crushing force of rejection.

There beneath the cool, midday sunshine of spring, within the midst of those young men, the Lord turned my attention toward *another* soul on the ranch who had known an entire lifetime of rejection.

"Boys, I need your help today," I began, as I started to verbally prepare them for what they were about to see. "We have a new horse on the ranch. She is the most severe rescue case we have ever seen." I continued to explain to them what she had been, what she was now, and…by God's grace…what she would become.

"She is just like you and me," I stated. "On the outside, she's a bit rough to look at, but her extraordinary inside is showing through more and more each day. Because she has *accepted herself how she is*…she's getting stronger and more beautiful by the minute."

I told the boys that I needed their help to continue her socialization process. "When you enter her paddock, remember that she is still recovering and is extremely shy. I would be so grateful if you would just stand very quietly and, if she chooses, allow her to come to you."

With their instructions firmly in place, the boys sauntered back toward her corral behind the arena. I held the gate open for them as they quietly stepped past me. Together, there were seven of us all standing in a vague semicircle. The group seemed a bit unimpressed as they stood as one waiting to help something they hadn't yet seen. They did not realize that she was resting in the shade of her wind shelter just beyond their view.

Moments seemed to silently blow by like lazy dandelion

spores. Amongst the young men, I could see the tiny yet unmistakable indications of their impatience beginning to rise. Mild irritation snuck out like escaping steam through the cracks of a big sigh, shifting weight, arms across chest, hands shoved in pockets, and nearly uncontrollable twitching. I smiled to myself as I recognized that for the young, simply "waiting" *can* be torture. Perhaps it isn't until we are older that we begin to fully realize how incredibly precious each moment of our life is. So much of the fullness of our lives comes from what we choose to see between the lines.

I looked over to see my true embodiment of "between the lines" peek around the wall of the wind shelter to see who had come to visit her. With the timid eyes of a doe, she pondered the boys for several moments. Then, like a nearly invisible mist moving over a river, barely seen and never heard, she silently ventured out of her security toward the boys.

All signs of irritation and impatience shattered like thin ice beneath the weight of her shocking presence. A long, low "Whoooooooooaaaaaa" slipped through the lips of one onlooker as he tried to comprehend the tortured creature that was approaching him.

In complete submission tinged with a hint of curiosity, she drifted toward our half sphere with her head lowered slightly and her eyes up. Like a shy lily reaching for the sun, she stretched her nose toward the boy closest to her.

After considering him for a moment, she reached out to another boy on the opposite side of our semicircle. As if collectively holding their breath, the boys stood in complete silence, instinctively holding very still. Their frozen posture indicated how sweetly evident it was that none of the boys wished to frighten this timid soul.

She carefully inspected every visitor in the group. After what appeared to be private contemplation, Phoebe gave the impression that she arrived at a definitive decision and then did something completely unexpected…she looked straight at Matt, stepped forward, and pressed her forehead flat against his chest!

I fully acknowledge that the mysteries of equine communication still baffle me at times. Of all those in the group, including myself…she chose Matt…the one most like her…the one that longed most for acceptance.

It was obvious that Matt didn't know what to do. Searching for what should be his reaction, his eyes shot between hers and mine. Finally, without a word, in an attempt to "pet" her, he raised his right hand and just sort of popped her on the top of the head a few times. Instantly, Phoebe threw her head out of harm's way and looked at him with very startled eyes!

One of the boys to my left tried to stifle a smirk. "Gently, Matt," I said. "Gently…quietly put your hand on her and just keep it there. Make small circles on her coat…she really loves that."

As Matt began to smooth his hands over the little horse, I could see the expression on his face begin to change. For him, the rest of the world just fell away. Here was a young man experiencing, perhaps for the first time, what it really meant to look and live between the lines. With as little disturbance as possible, I silently moved the rest of the boys out of the paddock.

She chose *him*. Out of everyone, he was the one that she sought out.

The tattered, rejected, love-starved horse choosing the tattered, rejected, love-starved boy. At this point, little else on the face of this earth honestly mattered. Love…had risen out of the dross, and like a stream through the desert, it trailed in its magnificent wake…life.

After the rest of the group moved to another area of the ranch, I retrieved a few brushes for Matt to use. Together, we groomed Phoebe for quite a while. Light conversation flowed easily between us. He, like the other boys, was engaging and polite as our dialogue meandered from one topic to another.

I glanced at him from time to time and noticed that his eyes never rose to meet mine. Instead, they stayed lowered, seemingly intent on not losing contact with this little horse. His manner revealed that perhaps he believed she was a phantom; just maybe, if he looked away…she would disappear. Not wishing for this moment to pass, his gaze remained locked like a laser on the fuzzy, bay target. With as few words as possible, I returned my brush to the white bucket at his feet and quietly backed up toward the gate. As if retreating from the room of a dozing infant, I didn't wish to disturb this extraordinary moment.

Because the boys had done such a wonderful job volunteering, I showed my clear appreciation by using a "secret" key to open the ranch soda machine, and let each of them help themselves to whatever flavor sounded best to them. While walking out of the main barn, I tied the arms of my fleece jacket firmly around my waist, evidence of the increasingly beautiful day.

It was nearly time for the boys to leave and head back to the facility. All had returned from their individual experiences on the ranch…except Matt. Upon minimal exploration, he was found in exactly the same place he had been left hours before…inside Phoebe's paddock with a brush in his hand, gently grooming her transitioning coat.

It took a great deal of persuasion…and nearly a crow bar to convince Matt to leave the small horse's side. With great hesitation, he joined me as I held the gate open, offering him to walk through it with me. He was not disrespectful in any way, but his body language clearly spoke: To leave this horse is *not* what he wished for.

Several days after Matt's unique visit, his counselor called me. "I have something that I need to share with you concerning Matt," she began. I could hear that her voice was strained, and immediately felt rising concern gather within my chest. "After his visit out to the ranch, Matt started to behave in a very uncharacteristic manner. I could easily see that his typical laid-back style had suddenly collided into a dam that was invisible to everyone but him. Everything about his demeanor shouted with a silent voice that he was suffering from some great, internal conflict."

She continued by recounting many failed attempts to encourage him to open the obviously pressurized flood gates of his soul. With stealthy evasion, he countered back with little more than an indication that she was right.

"He kept stalling by saying things like, 'I need to talk to you…but not now.' Or, 'I still want to talk to you…but not yet.' It wasn't until several days later, when we were finally able to sit down, that I realized he had been waiting for a quiet, semi-private time to talk."

A long pause passed between us in near silence. The only sounds I could hear over the phone were her failing attempts to win the battle for her crumbling composure. Finally, after a great sigh, she plunged forward.

"Kim, I watched as Matt slumped down in the chair before me. He grabbed the front of his shirt with his hand and began to stammer in a near whisper, 'My heart…my heart…something is happening to my heart!'"

I heard her voice completely break as she emotionally recalled, "His eyes filled with tears as he continued to clutch

the part of his shirt in front of his heart. Finally, he looked up
at me, and in a voice that I could barely hear, he said, 'I never
knew that I could be *loved*...I never knew that there was anyone on this earth who would believe in *me*...If the people and
the horses at that ranch on the hill can love me...and believe in
me...maybe it's time...for me to start *believing in myself*.'"

Tears of redemption began to fall.

In a single, quiet moment, the direction of Matt's life changed.

Love is like that. It soars above the boundaries we absently
confine it to. It breaks through what we mistake as unbreakable.
It redeems captives once thought unredeemable as it roars over
their crumbling dams of uncertainty. No matter what we might
observe on the surface, like an arrow that cannot be pulled out,
love's truth pierces the heart with undeniable permanence.

Before God...it never returns void.

It costs the giver nothing...it gives the receiver everything!
It is the most valuable treasure, worth far more than all the combined wealth the world has ever known...yet, it is free to give.

Whatever shape or presence it inhabits, love matters...per-
haps more than we know. Pure love, refined of all the dross the
world associates with it...truly changes our very foundations.

# 11

# The Prescription

Featured in the book *Hope Rising* is a truly distressing account of how despondent and grief-stricken this author has recently become. Because of being surrounded by a multitude of speedier paws, she never actually gets to eat any of the "Vitamin M's" (i.e., M&M's) that are so graciously donated to the ranch for her consumption. I know! I know! Just the thought of it makes my eyes well up too!

Apparently there were many more readers than I realized who know the incredible health benefits of "Vitamin M" and how vitally important it is to *not* fall into deficiency. Everyone knows that the documented and sometimes dangerous symptoms of "Vitamin M" deficiency include: violent mood swings, tantrums, depression, uncontrollable crying, and weight loss! These benevolent folks were obviously plagued…outraged, appalled, even sleepless…with the cruelty and unfairness of my continuing plight.

The incredible depth of their sympathy—and truly how *much* they could "feel my pain"—has recently been made known. Because of their mountainous generosity and humanitarian work, many of these blessed, benevolent souls have sought to ease my suffering. Whether it be through the mail, via carrier, or face to face, their relief efforts to stave off a "Vitamin M" deficiency here at the ranch have continued to pour in.

Morale on the ranch was at an all-time high when this author, after taking a weekend away from the ranch to mentally recover from her own personal deficiency, walked into the tack room only to stagger backward at the *colossal splendor* that was suspended within.

There…hanging on several bridle racks, dressed in all of their white-plastic-bagged magnificence…hung the objects of my affection. A true "Earth Angel" had graced my tack room with five grocery bags *full* of "Vitamin M." When all was counted, there, floating before me like a mirage…clothed in heavenly white…illuminated with shafted light from above… were *thirty-eight pounds* of "Vitamin M"! Be still my heart! And yes, I heard the angels singing too!

My season of drought was over! Rejoicing could be heard throughout the land! Never again would I suffer the torturous, unhealthy experience of going without my beloved "Vitamin M"! Thirty-eight pounds of chocolate bliss would become the very foundation to sustain a virtual oasis within my desert of lack.

*Holy cow!* Who am I trying to kid?! In the real world of distinguished chocolate consumers, thirty-eight pounds of chocolate would last…I don't know…maybe *fourteen years?* But that's in the real world…here on the ranch, it lasted exactly two and a half weeks…and that was only because we tried to *ration* it!

Doggone! Looks like I'm still out here in the desert of chocolatelessness. So, for all of my deeply compassionate sympathizers…keep on sympathizin'—because, from the looks of things…I'm gonna need it!

# 12

## Cleansing Fire

I t was only days after Christmas, and holiday warmth continued to envelope me in all that this remarkable time of year embodies. The sun slipped beneath the frozen horizon, embracing all creation with a final, golden, good-night kiss. The temperature dropped with the fading glory of the sky as the sun continued its retreat toward bed.

After working in my office long enough to feel the outside chill coming in, I decided it was a good time to nuke a mug of peppermint tea and find my favorite fleece blanket to wrap around my legs.

The familiar chirp from my kitchen proclaimed that my tea was ready. I followed the sound back into the other room while tying my fleece blanket under my arms like a sarong. Not wishing to trip, I was aware of the remainder of the blanket that was dragging across the hardwood floor behind me. Smiling to myself, I knew that it was most certainly dusting a new path, giving evidence of where my broom hadn't been in a while.

Once settled back into my chilly office, I was completely startled when the phone shattered the stillness around me. It was late…too late for a casual call. The tightness in my chest continued to grow as the unfamiliar male voice confirmed who I was. "Your number was relayed to us in case of an emergency.

Do you know Cheree and Jenna Smith?" I must have answered him affirmatively because he continued, "Ma'am, there has been a fire at the scene. Cheree and Jenna are unaccounted for. Can you come…?"

Horrifying thoughts rushed through my head. I was nearly certain Jenna had informed me earlier that she was going out with a group of her friends for a belated Christmas party at one of their homes. *Lord…where was Cheree?* As a hard-working single mother, Cheree usually enjoyed quiet evenings at home. "Did she go to bed early? What if she wasn't awakened by the fire? If she made it out of her home, the authorities would know that; she would be there with them. *Dear Jesus…*" My heart clenched in fear of the sickening picture that was beginning to take shape within my imagination.

They were a family of two; they needed each other intensely. I couldn't imagine one surviving without the other…and I didn't want to. As my mind continued to slip toward the unthinkable, I rationalized that no human being can replace another. *But, Lord, if you call me to, I am ready to open my arms, my heart, and my life to make a family…if theirs is no more.* The sheer weight of this possible outcome was not a scenario that I wanted to imagine, or even could.

In what felt like a single motion, I pulled on a pair of boots and a heavy coat while running across our frozen deck and down the fifteen steps into the garage. "Cheree and Jenna's house is on fire!" I yelled above the blaring radio as I burst in on Troy, who was working on an old car. In fast forward, we quickly navigated the seven miles of snowy road between our homes.

While my eyes strained to see beyond the truck's headlights through the darkness that lay before us, I couldn't help but replay how I first met Jenna and Cheree. Jenna had started coming to the ranch at the age of fourteen. She was the only child of her single and greatly devoted mother. Together they moved to Central Oregon for a new start, one which hopefully would nurture Jenna's growing passion for horses.

It was easy to see that horses were her release. In today's rapidly growing youth culture of super popularity and hyper-attention to appearance, style, and socializing, Jenna's acute shyness and lack of "conformity" left her with no friends of any duration. In the world of her peers, she was completely alone.

Horses became the true family of friends that she so ear-nestly sought. They always accepted her. They never taunted her for being a brilliant, straight-A "nerd." When she approached, they never ignored her. If she didn't don the latest style, they never snickered. When she was growing so lanky and tall, they never made fun of her. For Jenna, horses were always steadfast and loyal. They asked no questions; instead they chose to adopt her exactly as she was. They kept all her secrets and didn't ever tell another soul. They never let her down. In fact, they always bore her up, carrying her to a freedom that was unequalled anywhere else in her life.

With the horses on the ranch, it was obvious that she loved them…and they loved her. And that…was enough. On more than one occasion, while directing kids to find Jenna, I heard myself say, "Just look for the tallest girl on the ranch. She's slender with auburn hair, blue eyes…you'll find her with the horses…"

As the ranch reached out to her, she reached back. Jenna gave countless hours of volunteer time, summer after summer. When she outgrew her beloved-but-small horse, she donated Robby to the ranch so he could continue to rescue other little ones just as he had rescued her. With this girl, even from the beginning, it was always apparent that she was never about serving herself; she was clearly, visibly, and unmistakably about serving others.

With incredible determination, planning, and hard work, Jenna and her mother, Cheree, were able to purchase a little house outside of town. It was a "humble beginning," but it was *their* beginning. As a team, Cheree worked hard to provide the finances while Jenna was the young, strong back laboring to see all the chores to completion. Together they set about making their tired house…into a home.

When invited over for their "official" housewarming, the first thing I noticed when I entered through the front door was what appeared to be fragments of Jenna's life captured in still photographs. One photo featured a preschool-age Jenna with a tiny pony. Another group of photos showed the incremental stages of her grade-school years. Still another picture showed Jenna beaming with shy pride as she stood in front of Robby, her equine soul mate, while holding up what I assumed was the very first ribbon that they had won together.

In front of a worn, floral couch rested a lovingly crafted gift that I learned was made by Cheree's father. In what must have certainly taken a great deal of time, he had fashioned a coffee table made completely out of used horseshoes. Already it proudly displayed many keepsakes and artifacts of Jenna's early youth.

Nearly every wall presented an era of Jenna's burgeoning artistic adventures in a multitude of mediums. I couldn't help but notice and appreciate that in all their efforts to make this simple structure a home…they had truly succeeded.

Few could have been more proud of them both than Troy

and I. It was with utmost admiration and respect that we invited Jenna to "officially" become a part of our ranch staff. She had worked so hard for so long, and within this process had changed so much. The once silent girl, who had known vicious rejection and even verbal and physical threats from her high school contemporaries, against great difficulties continued to "stay the course" and graduate with honors.

Each season seemed to herald a new venue for her personal growth. Step by step, I watched in complete awe as she methodically found her voice, her purpose...her self. Truly my life was made more rich by watching her purposeful transformation from a shy, lonely girl into an engaging, active, beautiful young woman.

When it was time for her to enter college, true to her nature, she researched every detail. Because she worked hard to attain perfect grades and had applied for many scholarships, Jenna was able to find most of the funding for her first year. With the generous help of several organizations, her living expenses were also covered. Jenna...was going to college.

Unfortunately, the onset of her second year of college brought some bad news with it. The financial aid she had secured her first year was not going to be renewed. With great sadness, she came to me and expressed that she was going to land far short of the monetary help that she needed to reach for her dreams of attending college for another year.

What first appeared as a crushing blow, after much prayer, transformed into something remarkable—just as Jenna had. Her lack became the perfect place for the Lord to demonstrate His amazing love by pouring out help—just for her—from what some might consider impossible circumstances. Her goal, her hope, her dream crashed through what appeared to everyone as impenetrable odds…and became a reality. Her second year of college was provided through remarkable means…an envelope arrived at the ranch with nothing more than her name on the outside…and everything that she needed on the inside.

Troy's abrupt turn onto the dirt road that led to their home yanked my attention back to the present. We bounced through the winter-inspired maze of potholes and washboards as we climbed up the low hillside upon which their house rested. As we approached, we could see countless emergency vehicles all with their lights rotating ominously though the smoky darkness. Even from my distant vantage, it was obvious…their simple home was destroyed. The roof that had once sheltered their living room, dining room, and kitchen had been reduced to a yawning hole that encircled a glowing tower of menacing orange flames.

It was a chaotic scene. Firemen were streaming in and out of the front door. Some were struggling to drag in a water hose while others appeared to be dragging out completely destroyed "fuel items." These looked like bits and pieces of what used to be their furniture. The only fragment I could still recognize was the completely charred and partially denuded floral couch.

Troy jammed the truck into first gear and snapped off the key. I jumped out of the truck before it had completely stopped. A crowd had gathered and everyone seemed to be talking at once. I pushed my way through the milling group to a fireman and nearly shouted above the clamor, "Have you found the owners?" He cupped his ear in an attempt to better hear my question. I repeated it with more volume. He motioned toward another fireman and pointed, clearly indicating that he was the man in charge.

Panic began to rise in my throat as I scanned the gathering

crowd for Cheree and Jenna. They were no where to be found.

I ran to the fireman who had been indicated to me. I assumed he was the incident commander, and from a short distance I identified myself: "You just called me. My name is Kim Meeder. Do you have any word on Cheree and Jenna?"

As he strode toward me, I could see that he was talking on a cell phone in his right hand while giving various commands on the radio gripped in his left. I felt like I was shouting above the bellowing fire hoses and radios just to be heard. Wordlessly, by simply holding up one index finger, he asked me to stop.

A virtual lifetime was passing through my thoughts as I waited. *Where are they?* I wondered as I lingered in the darkness. The flames that knifed through the roof were subsiding now. The firemen, who were now covered with soot, continued to move in and out of what was now the burned-up shell of my friends' home. There was no rush or urgency in their movements.

Cheree and Jenna could *not* still be inside...they would know by now. The firemen's actions told me that the building was cleared. That's why they called me...because they *don't* know where they are. A weak wave of relief moved through me as I reasoned that they were *not* inside but somewhere else... safe.

The fireman's hand lowered as he stepped toward me again. His face registered an awkward mix of stress, fatigue, and relief. He pulled in a deep breath and exhaled in a flurry of white. "It has been confirmed that Cheree and Jenna are spending Christmas with their family three hours away in Portland."

I, too, exhaled in a flurry of white breath. They were safe... for now, that was all that truly mattered.

On our return trip home, I couldn't even begin to fathom

what it would be like to lose *everything*. Yes, one might say that they are only "things," but they are all the intrinsic things that have unique value to us. I pondered the fact that I keep the last ten years of photographs under my bed, my grandmother's bowls in my kitchen, one of my mother's few remaining oil paintings in the living room, and an entire dresser filled with countless gifts, cards, and letters from my "extended family" from all over the United States and beyond. Yes, they are all just "things"—not one of which I could ever imagine being replaced. These "things" represent little bits and pieces of us— our life and our history.

Even though insurance would cover some of their "hard costs," I tried to understand the magnitude of the sense of loss that my dear friends were soon to face.

*Lord, they worked so hard to make this little house theirs. They filled it with simple treasures that made it a home...their home. What they had was not a lot to begin with...and, yet, they lost it all. Lord...why them?*

Later, when I spoke with Cheree and Jenna, the magnitude of their loss was etched in a nearly wordless expression of pale shock. The enormity of this event was completely overwhelming. Cheree clearly summed it all up when she whispered, "Where do we go from here?".

In the following aftermath, Cheree revealed that one of the hardest moments was driving up to what used to be their home and finding instead a blackened "junkyard" of what used to be their belongings. "On one side of the yard was my mattress. On the other side was the couch. Not far from it was a pile of burned up chairs. It was just so surreal." Jenna mirrored her sense of loss by adding, "It really wasn't until we started the clean-up process that I began to find bits of my life in the ash...a chip from some pottery that I made in high school, half a page of a special note that my mom wrote for me, a piece of a treasured toy that I had saved from childhood. So much of it was from things that I had forgotten I even had. Examining each irreplaceable piece was like 'marathon grieving,' because every fragment came from something that had special value and meaning."

No tragedy makes sense at the time, some even less than others. If this would have happened to a family that had more resources, more ability to rebound, more financial cushioning, it might have seemed a bit more "fair." Yet this had happened to a little family that was existing on one income. Now, all that they had was completely gone.

It is in times like these that I realize how fully limited my view of the "big picture" really is. I would have never chosen this for my friends. Thankfully, I don't get to choose the pathway for those I love. What a miserable harbinger I would be...I can't even see five minutes into the future! These are the times when I am so incredibly grateful that God is truly in control. The tapestry of life that He is creating from my perspective often looks like an impossible tangle of knots and threads with no design, they don't seem to match or make much sense. Yet, God's perspective is something incredible, rational, and complete. He sees the tapestry from above—how every thread aligns with every other thread to create purpose, value, meaning, and transcending beauty.

I have seen this to be true my whole life. We ask God to guide our life...and He *does*...just never in ways that we *expect*. He sees the whole picture, and like any loving father, understands that our greatest treasures rise from our greatest depths.

For many months to follow, my friends traveled a path that seemed far too steep for any single mother and daughter to navigate. Every foundational and minute detail of their lives had to be reordered and reestablished. In a very short amount of time, every answer to every question about how to provide for today and begin rebuilding for tomorrow came from one physically and emotionally *exhausted* woman.

While Cheree's bank and insurance company fought with each other over what the burned-out family should do, she was required to jump through their tangled maze of conflicting hoops in a desperate attempt to just see past the present. During this time, Cheree confided to me that she was so crushed between their contradictory requirements that at times she feared her family would receive no help at all.

They had to change, they had to adapt, they *had* to grow. As their steps carried them higher into never-before-seen territory, slowly their view began to change.

The scattered shards of their former life began to rearrange into a picture far more beautiful than the one they had become so accustomed to. As only God can, when we ask Him, He crafts our wreckage into something usable, whole, and redeeming. The fire that destroyed…also became the fire that cleansed. It burned away all the tangle that perhaps was blocking their view of what was God's *best* for them.

An empathetic businesswoman gathered all of her friends

together and purchased everything—emphasis on *everything*—that Cheree and Jenna would need for a new kitchen. All but one of these women were complete strangers. Immediate financial donations came from everywhere...even from folks that they did not know personally. One of Jenna's friends used the gift cards that she had received for Christmas and spent them—all of them—on Jenna so she would have some new clothing. To ease Jenna's first night back in town, many of her friends gathered around her to create as much "familiarity" as they could in an attempt to soften her transition into the unknown. Several different neighbors took care of their dogs and horses, helping to provide for their long-term needs. Later, a large group of friends and family gathered to help clean the property of all that had been destroyed.

Through all of this...Cheree's perspective about "tragedy" began to change. She told me later, "A fire destroyed our home...but created something new, something completely unexpected. Loss reveals what is truly important. Our house was gone...but we were not...we could go on. Instead of seeing the charcoaled property that used to be my home...I saw how many had extended themselves to help us...I saw how much I was completely...*loved*." Cheree's voice thinned into a near whisper beneath the weight of truth that streaked down her cheeks.

Once their new home was built, it was there—while sprawled on the floor like dominos, watching a fun surfing documentary with more than twenty of Jenna's friends—I suddenly realized that all they had been through, everything they had survived... suddenly came into sharp focus. Here, mashed into this beautiful new home—filled with stocking-footed teenagers, ranch staff, and volunteers—brightness, laughter, and life was as palatable as the Mountain Dew and popcorn. It was official: Their new home could not hold more joy!

Above the happy, tangled jumble, I looked over at Cheree and smiled. Her returned expression of contentment supported everything that I was only now realizing. Even from across the room, I could see that there was "knowing" in her eyes...*this* is what it was all about.

I suddenly felt like someone who had just walked in on their own surprise party...*Ah ha!* Now all the previously known pieces of truth concerning my friends had come together to make a clear picture...crystal clear.

Quite suddenly, it all made sense.

———|·|———

*Young Wisdom*

Rebecca, age 23: "Faith is just like the mountains;
even when it's dark or foggy and we can't see them...
it doesn't change the fact that they're still there."


Abby, age 10, after toppling off of a
cantering horse, standing up, and brushing off:
"Hey! Am I a *cowgirl* yet?"

# 13

## Perspective

It was a gorgeous day in November. Rising like a bearer of good news, brilliant sunshine flooded the high desert in unseasonable warmth. The unusually balmy fall had exalted ordinary trees into a visual symphony of explosive color. I couldn't help but admire the dazzling examples that surrounded the ranch as I turned onto the dirt drive that led up the hill to the office, which we lovingly call the Bunkhouse.

As I have done for the last dozen years, I slowed to look at the remarkable family of horses that continue to bless my life and all who travel up this road. Absorbing every bit of the mid-morning sun, nearly the entire herd was cast in their favorite napping position. Most were standing with their eyes half mast and heads hung low. Several more were lying down on their chests while resting their chin on the ground, and a few were completely sacked out on their sides, eyes shut and mouths open, snoring away.

*What a picture of incredible bliss*, I thought to myself. They certainly deserved it, each having worked so remarkably hard that season. *To just lie in the sun...what could be better than that?* I thought. Like smoke lifting from a gathering fire, a silly wisp of envy rose within me. *That is truly what I long for, Lord...just a moment to lie down in the sun for a little while.*

It had been a season with no equal. Never had I experienced such an extended period of acute "time compression." For months, I had been cajoling myself with the rationale that my life was just really full of good stuff…a *lot* of good stuff. The ranch riding program would be closing for the season in a few days, and there was so much to finish. I had traveled to more speaking and media engagements this season than all other years combined, and my time away had resulted in a virtual landslide of paperwork so deep I could barely open my office door…and only a handful of weeks remained to write another book. All good stuff…just a *lot* of good stuff.

My normal "Go, Kim, Go" had either left without me or I left without it. Perhaps it was still up the hill, tucked snugly in bed, which is really where I wanted to be.

I was so intensely exhausted that my body felt remarkably heavy and disconnected from my head. My schedule had reduced my sleep threshold to far below what is optimal for my head to function well. With immense concentration, and lots of coffee, I felt that I was barely able to focus well enough to drive safely. At this point, I wondered if I was truly able to operate a stapler…let alone work with a horse and child. Even though these are *extremely* rare days for me, I still found it difficult to admit that I was just absolutely worn out.

My nurturing staff—who I love so much—completely agreed. "Girl, you just need to go and do something mindless for a while, okay?" Their generosity, in the face of their own great fatigue, humbled me to the ground. I was fully aware that what they were actually saying in effect was "We'll shoulder your load along with ours so you can rest a bit."

With my pockets full of staples, a roll of chicken wire under each arm, and a hammer in my hand…I set out with Rebecca to go and wrap trees. We were getting ready to move our young horses into their winter paddock, which had many large juniper trees that needed added protection from their mischievous little teeth.

Rebecca had also been banished with me to "mindless land" because she was sadly losing her race of trying to outrun the flu. Even though it had also been an extraordinary season for the ranch staff, each individual was struggling with their own sense of exhaustion to finish it as well as they could.

The time spent with Rebecca beneath the juniper trees was a welcome reprieve for both of our weary hearts. She is such a remarkable young woman that even in sickness, no difficult day could rival her intrinsic joy. Our conversation mimicked the random, drifting pattern of the clouds that moved over the mountains behind us. I welcomed the peaceful, rare moment of quiet to learn more about her volunteer efforts to help a struggling youth group in the community just north of the ranch.

Her recounting of the details was serenaded by the intermittent squeals and laughter from two high-school-age girls nearby. I could clearly see that Melissa and Sarah, each volunteering, seemed to be more effective at wrapping each other with wire instead of the trees. Even though it was already a warm day, their combined hilarity made it even more so.

In my sadly deteriorated state, I was only vaguely aware that Troy was giving one of his very first "official" tours of the ranch. Normally I would have accompanied him, but on this day, I would have been far more of a detriment than a help. I felt so thin, so stretched…not unlike a rubber band reaching around far too many things. I knew that my long-term, well-intended efforts to support more, on this day, created just the opposite. My positive objective to do more had actually driven me to do much less. My life, instead of flowing like a great river, had been reduced to an insignificant gurgle.

*Lord, I know that Your strength never runs out. Instead of operating in Your strength...have I been unknowingly operating in mine? Your truth is unchanging...while my emotion is...*

My thoughts trailed off as I noticed an unfamiliar woman carefully make her way through the corral toward me. She was clutching a book that I was guessing she wished for me to sign. Slowly I extricated myself from the roll of wire around my hands and backed down the teetery ladder on which I stood.

As she approached, I noticed that she was older and very small. Her movements were well chosen and purposeful. Simply walking through the paddock toward me did not seem to be an easy task for her. I excused myself from the girls and took several steps in her direction.

She greeted me with great apology for her "interruption" of my day, and indeed asked if I would mind signing her well-worn book. While she searched her pockets for a pen, I engaged her by asking many questions about her home and her time spent here on the ranch. She began to gush about Troy and how special this place was, as she finally located her stray pen and handed it to me. As I began to write, she shared how she had actually tried to come to the ranch earlier in the summer but was too ill to make the trip... "You see, I have terminal cancer..."

My pen stopped.

"But today is a really good day, actually a wonderful day," she said, as she continued to explain how she should have passed away long ago.

Still kneeling down with her open book balanced on my thigh, truth thundered into my heart like a herd of galloping drafts.

Here I had been so focused on my own "problem," my own exhaustion...which few have ever perished from...that I nearly missed the bigger picture. Suddenly, when cast against such blackness, how clear the truth of God became. While I was muddling around in *my own* personal fog, seeking only to fulfill *my own* immediate needs, God, in His wisdom, sent a very powerful message to shatter *my own* private misconception...

As I stood up, I looked directly at this pocket-sized woman. There, beaming from beneath her cute straw hat was an expression so radiant that it was only then that I noticed that she was indeed...bald. Although she was facing one of the greatest challenges known in this life, she was bright. In truth, she was brighter than bright. She was literally shining with hope. Instead of succumbing to her pain, she bloomed within it. She was a *dying* woman giving hope...and perspective...to a *tired* woman.

While the impact of her presence continued to cascade into my soul, I asked her if she would be kind enough to allow me the honor of praying for her.

Her quiet account of her illness suddenly stopped as she looked at me with remarkably clear blue eyes. She exhibited the same stunned silence as someone who has just won something of great value. In her unabashed delight, she was quicker than I was. While I was still reaching for her hands, she dodged my offer and ducked beneath them, choosing instead to snuggle in under my arm. Like a child cuddling into the comfort of her mother, she pressed herself below my arm and rested her head against my chest. Now, it was *I* who truly felt like the one who had just won something of great value…for, most certainly, I truly had.

In that moment of simple, unequalled honor, I could feel the snowflakes of blessing begin to fall. While buried beneath their resilient drift, I became the most blessed woman on earth.

There, praying under the junipers, with the embodiment of hope nestled under my arm, I realized what the greater picture is, and just how very close I had come to missing it completely.

I was nearly lost in my dull and selfish state when I realized how sometimes we can become so focused on our own needs that we step right over the very people God has sent to rebuild us.

Neither places, times, or things restore people as much as *people* restore people.

We need each other. Not only when we're exhausted…but *especially* when we're exhausted. When we become stressed and drained, instead of running away…perhaps we should think about running *toward*. Something remarkable happens to our hearts when we serve one another. There is little else in this world that changes us more. Just ask any volunteer and watch their eyes; the immediate sparkle will shout this truth.

When overwhelming times come in ways that look and feel like our imminent destruction, turning inward rarely heals us as much as...turning outward. It's only when we have given to the point of exhaustion that we truly can understand and experience the remarkable wonder that it is to receive.

In reality, suffering and blessing balance on the same high wire, each giving stability and depth to the other. The one that we feel the most...is ultimately the one that we give the most.

How we feel eventually returns to where our focus is... truly, it's just a matter of perspective.

# 14

# A Dog's Tale

Kathy is part of our much loved staff at the ranch. She is truly a rare jewel of a woman whose friendship is so genuine that just being around her always leaves my life more rich and full. No matter how much time goes by or how great the physical distance is between us, her loving companionship in my heart remains unchanged.

As often as we are able to do so throughout the season, Troy and I try to schedule a few well-deserved "rest trips" for our staff. It was during one such trip to the Oregon Coast that Kathy and I decided to go jogging on the beach. Side by side, with near unison strides, we led our shadows down a particularly beautiful stretch of sugary sand. Overhead, the sky imitated the waves below by tossing gleaming white clouds among a brilliant blue current. Easy conversation accompanied the soft rhythm of our feet drumming over the beach.

Kathy is highly skilled in many areas, including her incredible capacity to run. Typically she is a gazelle in running shoes and has expertly paced me through many marathons. But on this particular day, I sensed something was distracting her, something heavy…very heavy. Finally, I asked her plainly, "Kath, what's wrong?"

We jogged on in silence for what seemed like a long

stretch. She was visibly struggling to find the strength for what she needed to say. I could literally feel her anguish making its way to the surface. I watched in sorrow as my precious friend lost her struggle for composure. In awkward silence I followed her weakening strides until she slowed to a walk. Her crumbling gaze fell only moments before she tightly closed her large green eyes. Like a child's sand castle surrendering to a breaching wave, she collapsed into the powdery beach. "Oh, Kim," she faltered as her soft voice broke… "Calvin died."

My heart felt as if it had been pierced by an arrow of fire. She had loved that little black dog like a child. As the realization of her loss seared within, I sunk into the sand beside her and pulled her close. Her entire body convulsed in wave after wave of agonizing sorrow. There on the beach, we held each other through her private storm. Around us, as they have for all time, the waves of the sea continued their ancient rhythm. The wind was still blowing the sand into intricate patterns. Traveling on an unseen path, the clouds coursed over head, until they were silently swept out of our sight. The cycle of life continued on, but for two figures bent in grief on a windswept beach, everything stopped.

Calvin had been Kathy's first—and only—dog. Before I met her, she had survived an extremely tumultuous time in her life. It was during that difficult era that her only true and constant pillar had been the devotion of that little Labrador cross. His unwavering love had become the light in her darkness that drew her through one of the bleakest seasons she had ever known.

Slowly we made our way to a washed-up log and sat together as Kathy shared with me in broken sentences what had happened. Apparently, at the end of a family gathering, during the bustling departure, Calvin had been crushed beneath a car. The raw images slowly fell from her pale lips. She stammered through a description of the dog's screaming agony, their frantic trip to the vet...realizing she *had* to make the unthinkable decision...and then summoning the courage to say a final goodbye. The needle was inserted. While holding his mangled body, Kathy could think only of how much she loved and would miss this true and treasured companion. She kissed Calvin as his life slipped away...and then...he was gone.

Her canine soul mate was no more. With my chin resting on the top of her head, all I could do was hold my friend as her storm of grief raged.

---

Apart from our work at the ranch, Troy and I both have other jobs. Troy also works as a landscape contractor. He is half of an incredibly busy two-man team that works extraordinarily hard to fulfill the needs of the clients they serve. Shortly after our coast trip with the staff, he was hired to install an irrigation system for a new house being built in a very affluent housing development. All the homes were not only beautiful, but of gargantuan proportions as well. Most were boasting nearly every amenity that money could buy. Many of these spectacular houses were vacation homes that were left vacant for most of the year.

For Troy, it was a very pleasant place to work. Here, fences were prohibited, so that each yard flowed seamlessly into the next. This gave the lovely illusion that all yards and gardens were bigger than they truly were. Where one yard ended and another began was not easily discernable. Because of this unique feature, while mapping out the new property for trenches,

Troy vaguely noticed an apparently empty cage that was in the expansive backyard of the unoccupied house next door. Several days later, as he was working in the same area, a small movement caught his eye, and he realized that the distant cage, in fact, was not empty at all.

As we so often do, while preparing for supper that evening, Troy casually began to recount for me the events of his day. The more he spoke, the more the realization of what he had actually discovered began to burn within him. I could clearly see that something he had experienced during work had greatly shaken him.

Troy shared with me how he had discovered that the cage in the neighboring backyard was *not* empty. Because the massive house looked vacant, he was driven by his concern that whatever creature locked inside might be in need of care. Troy had first knocked on the front door of the house, but as expected, received no response. Next his investigation took him around to the backyard again. He needed to take a closer look at the cage which was no bigger than a large coffee table. To his great surprise, the tiny cage held a dog…a large female dog…and what looked like several months' accumulation of her feces. As Troy approached the cage, the obviously frightened dog shrank back, cowering into the furthest corner.

Evidently someone had been giving her food and water, because her weight was normal. Otherwise, she couldn't have been more horribly neglected. According to Troy, it appeared that she had tried to confine her waste to one corner of her cage, but the pile had grown so high that it had toppled over. Now, there was no where for her to lie down in this miserable little prison that wasn't covered with the ground-up, smashed-together, stinking mattress of excrement. The dog was soiled with filth; her black coat was matted with discharge that was oozing from what looked like a skin infection. Her belly hung in loose balding folds from her atrophied body.

Troy continued to recount his feelings of concern and anger and how they compelled him to become a man of action. Slowly, his compassion drew him to kneel beside her cage while comforting her with his voice. The terrified dog did not move from her original position.

Yet *hope cannot be denied*. After long moments of Troy gently talking to her, there was an infinitesimal change...a barely perceptible movement. Not unlike an old porch swing beginning to sway in the afternoon breeze. Her tail...began to move. With great caution, Troy curled his fingers through the wire mesh to reach her. Very slowly, with great hesitation, she began to edge shyly toward him. She carried her head and tail very low in complete submission to him as she timidly began to lick his fingers. With the wariness of a little mouse venturing out into the unknown, she tentatively pressed her cheek against his fingertips. Without hesitation, Troy scratched her greasy face. Soon, she was pressing her neck, her shoulder, her entire body against the wire mesh, trying to receive every bit of affection that Troy offered.

Her body language whispered that loving rain was falling into her desert of loneliness. She yielded as much of herself as possible to the flood before the drought returned. Her eyes transformed into deep brown pools of pure liquid gratitude, imploring Troy to never leave.

Troy stayed with her as long as he could before returning to work. He shared with me how the rest of the day his heart could not escape the images of the captive dog as he pondered her situation.

After Troy concluded his recounting, we discussed the possible options for the dog's future well-being. One thing became absolutely clear: Although we already had two very active dogs on the ranch, we would bring this one home immediately if the owners would be willing to relinquish her. Troy resolved to do everything he could to contact them and tactfully plead for her release.

The following day, as the ranch started to hum with activity, my heart was still heavy with mental images of the caged dog. My thoughts were interrupted by Kathy calling out to some kids as she strolled around the tack room and readied herself for another busy day. A bolt of lightning to the top of my head would have had less impact than the instantaneous idea that flashed across my mind. In an unexpected onslaught of jumbled words, I poured out to Kathy the story of the neglected dog.

She listened intently with guarded excitement. It was clear that she, too, would love to take this dog home. But as of yet, she didn't know how her new husband would respond to an addition so quickly after their tragic loss. As newlyweds, Kathy completely understood the shared respect and strengthening value of making important decisions together. A husband supporting his wife, a wife supporting her husband, each reaching across their own will to make the other stronger…this is what they both had promised to do.

Immediately, a bucket of ice water doused my enthusiasm as I sudden realized just how much I might have unintentionally hurt my friend. *Kim! What have you done?* I thought with shrinking sadness. What if the owners refused to give up their dog? My heart sank, and I instantly regretted telling Kathy about the dog's miserable plight. Would this become one more blow to her already-crushed spirit? *What an idiot!* I thought of myself. I could hardly believe how incredibly thoughtless I had just been to someone who truly needed my comfort. My rambling description of a horrible situation undoubtedly raised more unnecessary pain for her. Thankfully, our conversation was mercifully interrupted by the arrival of several more children who were eager to begin their various adventures at the ranch.

Several days passed as Troy tried with great futility to reach the dog's owners. Sadly, I could see that Kathy had cautiously settled her heart in a field of emotional land mines that I had inadvertently planted. It was painfully clear that she wanted desperately to know if we had heard anything about the needy dog, but was too afraid of having her hopes shattered to ask. I was aware that she had not yet talked to her husband, because of the great probability that the dog would never be released. Feeling miserable that I had added to her sorrow, I resigned myself to pray…pray for my friend's brokenness to be healed.

Quietly, sadly, one day slipped into another…still with no word about the dog.

Once again, Kathy and I were together stride for stride. We were pacing the halls of the local hospital in between the contractions of a friend who was in labor with her first baby. A nurse with dark circles under her eyes approached me and asked if my husband's name was Troy. I took the call in the maternity ward. His voice was literally bursting with excitement, and he was talking so fast that I could barely understand him. What I did make out was that he had finally reached the owners of the imprisoned dog and they had decided to give her up! He had the dog *with him* in the truck and was on his way home. His hasty plan was to swing by the pet store and buy the things she would need to start her new life, including a blanket and a collar. Then he was going to give her a thorough bath with a fragrant shampoo. "I want to make her as beautiful as I can, and then surprise Kathy with her today at the hospital," he said with great enthusiasm. Then he asked, "What do you think?"

Taking into full account my recent blunder, I answered with cautious hope, "I think that would make two miracles in one day."

Because she had been having contractions all night, our exhausted and laboring friend was napping sporadically when Troy arrived at the hospital. Without saying a word, he motioned for Kathy and me to silently slip from the maternity room and follow his beckoning arm toward the main exit. Once outside, he turned to Kathy and said simply, "I have a surprise for you."

Blinking hard in the intensely bright sunlight, she shaded her eyes and looked up into Troy's face. He smiled broadly. Sudden realization coursed through her like a wave. *She knew*. Her mouth parted slightly in shocked amazement as she continued to stare at Troy's face…perhaps searching for some sign that he was joking. Not brushing off her expectation with laughter, Troy instead offered her his elbow, like a groom leading his bride. I walked behind them, grateful to take in the moment as they strolled arm in arm through the parking lot toward his truck. With intense thankfulness and relief, I watched Kathy move closer, step by step, toward what I hoped would be the healing of her broken heart.

With great ceremony, Troy slowly opened the truck door. Together, we were greeted with the strong scent of damp dog and flowery shampoo. The newly released black Lab sat huddled on the floor under the dash, fresh from her bath. Her gaze seemed to shift back and forth between her front feet. She truly didn't know where to look. Undoubtedly this beleaguered dog was overwhelmed with the sudden compassion being poured into her life. She wore a new collar, decorated in Hawaiian style to match her new name. "Kathy," Troy said, "this is Ano. Her name is Hawaiian for *kind*."

Instinctively, Kathy bent down to the truck's floor level. "Oh, baby girl," she breathed, gently coaxing the timid dog toward her. Daring not to raise her head, Ano lifted only her eyes to look at Kathy. Still in a posture of complete submission, her gaze began to lengthen as she considered the new woman calling her. Faintly, like a near whisper, her tail started to hesitantly thump against the floor of the truck. With great caution, as she had with Troy, Ano slowly crept across the floor toward the gentle voice that beckoned her toward a new life. In moments, Ano had trusted Kathy enough to be enticed out of the confined safety of the truck toward the grassy, green islands that encircled the parking lot. As I followed them, I couldn't help but wonder how long it had been since Ano's paws had known the fresh softness of grass.

Kathy gently knelt beside her new charge. In total surrender, Ano collapsed and rolled over, revealing her hideous belly. Kathy's eyes didn't seem to notice the ugly folds of damaged skin. She saw only a canine heart pleading to be loved. Healing is Kathy's gift, and it flowed from her like a rising river. In a world that was filled with only a woman and a dog, Kathy breathed, "Ano, you're so beautiful...so beautiful." Her lips were close to the dog's chest; it appeared as if she was speaking directly to Ano's heart, ensuring that the truth she spoke would not go unheard. Without listening to the rest of her private conversation, just the tone of her voice alone was a convincing promise that a new season was coming.

Later, with Ano safely settled in Kathy's car, we went back

into the hospital to witness the second miracle of the day—the birth of our friend's perfect baby girl. When we finally said good-bye, our hearts were completely saturated with all of the profound fulfillment we had experienced in such a short amount of time. But as we walked out to our vehicles, Kathy confided to me that she still had one more bridge to cross. She still needed her husband Mark's support and approval to bring Ano into their home.

Troy and I had lovingly ambushed Kathy with the sudden responsibility of a new dog. And even though it had been the fulfillment of a dream for her, she understandably didn't want her husband to feel trapped by the same surprise. Arriving home late at night with a large, ragged-coated, sore-ridden adult dog—even a clean one—was not the most ideal way to present her case.

Although she had tried many times throughout the day, Kathy had not been able to reach Mark to speak to him about the possible "new addition." Because she wished to have this conversation face to face, the best she could think of was to leave him a message regarding "something important we need to talk about" when she got home.

When she finally pulled into the driveway, it was very late. She looked up to see that the light was on upstairs. As she had requested, Mark had faithfully waited up for their "big talk." She parked the car and took a deep breath. While gripping the steering wheel, she wondered what she could possibly say to make any of this sound like a good idea. She sincerely wanted what was best for the dog, but even more she wanted what was best for her and Mark. They were a team, and she would honor and respect him and his decision for them as a new family.

Finally, after gathering all of her gear and getting out of the car, she simply prayed that the Lord would lead the way.

With one arm full of groceries and doggy necessities and the other corralling a timid-yet-excited dog, she tried to *quietly* negotiate her way through the front door. Mark, who had been reading upstairs, called out a greeting to his exhausted wife…and began to notice conspicuously muffled sounds coming from the entryway. Suddenly, Kathy's fragile balancing act began to collapse. Ano pulled the leash from Kathy's hand. As she lunged for the dog, one of the grocery bags toppled out of her grasp and everything within it tumbled out and went spinning across the floor. The familiar sound of dog claws skittering across tile rose up the stairwell. Ano jumped up the stairs… alone…toward Mark. *What a disaster!* shot through Kathy's brain as she quickly clamored over the spilled groceries in a failed attempt to stop Ano. It was too late.

Kathy bounded up the stairs two at a time and reached the top to see that Ano had already found Mark. Again in complete submission, Ano had laid down over the top of his feet. She was in the process of surrendering her raw, ugly belly to him for stroking.

Mark looked up from petting the dog, and said with a surprised smile, "Is this what you wanted to talk about?"

Kathy saw her husband's eyes reflecting the same warmth that she had in the first moments of contact with Ano.

Mark knew how much his wife had suffered from the death of her little black companion, Calvin. He was aware of the cavernous hole that her tremendous loss had left behind. And no matter what the story was behind this grossly neglected creature, he understood how entirely important this dog was to the woman he loved.

"Honey…this is Ano…" Kathy began, fully recognizing

that this introduction was not going at *all* the way she had planned it. Mark's gaze dropped from Kathy back to the prone dog on top of his feet. He seemed to be studying her for long moments. Then, without looking up...Mark quietly spoke directly to the dog and simply said, "Welcome home Ano... welcome home."

———⊣⊢———

*Young Wisdom*

Brian, age 4: "You know what
I want to be when I grow up?
*A man.*"

# 15

# May Day

As far back as I can remember, the first day of May, or May Day, was always an excuse to love my grandma with flowers. She was an avid gardener, and flowers were always one of her favorite things. Even before my parents' death, before Grandma's home became mine, I remember how important this day was for us both.

It began when I was seven years old and continued for the next thirty-four years until she passed away.

Originally, I remember yanking handfuls of wadded-up yellow buttercups out of what was later to become a horse pasture and mashing them into an old mason jar full of water. The trick was to do a "mission impossible" up to the front door of the house, leave the flowers on the doormat, ring the doorbell, then run like a wild animal into the grapevines that grew on a low fence around the front yard. I discovered early on that this was one of the best places to hide while still being able to peek through the dense leaves and see her honest reaction to such random kindness.

The game continued, without fail, though grade school, middle school, junior high, high school, college, marriage, more college, careers, sports—every season in my life was metered and grounded by this one simple, annual event that was just between us. May Day always represented my little "stake in the sand" opportunity to gather flowers for my grandmother and somehow get them to her doorstep without ever being seen or caught.

I am certain that on many occasions the neighbors had a good laugh at the adult granddaughter of their elderly neighbor who lived across the way. Watching a grown woman dressed head to toe in black, diving from bush to tree to rock until she was able to belly-crawl to the front door and leave flowers…and then run away like her backside was on fire! It makes me laugh out loud to think that I did that *every year* for thirty-four years!

Part of the game was that since she never caught me, technically, she never could really be truly sure that the flowers were from me. She knew they were, and I knew she knew. But she could never actually *prove* it…which always gave us reason to laugh together.

Finally, at the generous age of eighty-nine, it was time for my precious grandma to go home. She died in August, the month I was born. Somehow, this "coincidence" has continually given me great comfort. For me, it has always felt like a "passing of the torch": "Honey, now it is *your* turn to run the race. Enjoy every moment, carry a smile on your face, the truth of Christ in your heart, and flowers in your hand…" For all that she had sacrificed for me, it is not an impression that I will ever be without.

As with everyone who has suffered great personal loss, it is no secret that the following year can be marked by many painful "firsts." The first Thanksgiving, the first Christmas, the first birthday, and for me the most painful was coming…the first May Day. This was our *special* day, a silly, symbolic pact between us celebrated by a goofy little thing I did so she would always be reminded of how much I loved her.

Grieving is a process as unique as each individual. I have also experienced that within this "course of action," every individual at some point has the ability to literally choose "action." For those who are dealing with loss, grieving can lead either to anger, brokenness, and continuing personal destruction, or we can *choose* for it to lead to joy, fullness, and continuing personal growth.

My little grandma was one of the happiest people I had ever known. *Lord, life is short...I choose joy*, I thought with resolve. *Yes, this was a very special time for us. Lord...show me how I can continue to pass that gift on*, I pondered as the days proceeded toward the first of May. *I guess that a solution will present itself*, I conceded when no great, concrete ideas suddenly materialized.

A few days later, it was early morning and I was hustling to gather my keys, jacket, and water bottle, grab my cell phone, and rush out the...I nearly stepped right on them! There they were...sitting on my door step...smiling up at me...a beautiful basket full of bright yellow flowers...

Everything stopped.

The cool air of morning rushed in all around me as I just stood there holding the door open. On this day, as there had been nearly all my life, lay flowers on a doorstep. Only this year...they were on *my* doorstep. I couldn't move. I just couldn't believe someone else would understand or really even care that this was a little gesture that had great personal value to *me*. But someone did...

Standing in the doorway, with early morning light as my witness, I slowly knelt down...picked the flowers up...held them to my chest...and cried. "Oh, Grandma...if you only knew..."

To this day, every May first, flowers mysteriously appear on the deck in front of my door. I have no idea who the giver might be. I have never seen them, nor have they ever been caught. I have always wondered, whoever it might be, if they really understand the incredible gift they have blessed my life with by helping to keep my grandma's memory close. I wonder if they know how truly special it is to be remembered in such a personal way. I wonder if they know that because of their remembrance...in this heart...something remarkable has happened.

Being remembered feels good. It reminds us that we are special to someone. The size or quantity of the "remembrance" really isn't as important to us as the fact that...we just are.

Many psychology studies have concluded over and over again that one of the greatest driving forces of the human heart...is simply to be needed.

To need another person should beget thanking them as well. Sometimes we can do that in uniquely simple ways. And if we are faithful in this endeavor...every now and then, something remarkable happens.

# 16

## *Bruises*

B ruises are evidence of where subdural bleeding has occurred. They are visual and often painful reminders of blows we have received. But unlike wounds, bruises do not leave scars. In time, deep purple turns into a rainbow of blue, violet, pink, and sometimes even a strangely beautiful yellowish green. Eventually our natural skin color returns and we are to the outside world "back to normal." Yet, like our scars, our bruises can teach us so much more than just about pain.

I had great reason to think about the bruising blows I had received in my own life as I hiked alone one afternoon through the Cascade wilderness. While making my way up the eastern flank of a ridge toward a connecting pass, my rising footsteps were measured with nearly rhythmic "crunches" as my boots broke through the crusty snow of early spring. With the air temperature already in the twenties and rising fast, combined with the crystal blue skies overhead, this certainly qualified as one of the first "bluebird" days of the year.

As the top of the ridge rounded into view, I could feel the typical northwest air flow ruffle my clothing. It was nearly time to pray.

*Lord, I have so many questions…* My thoughts were completely interrupted as the power of the Three Sisters Mountains towered into my view. *God, You are so amazing…* Once I found a special place to be still, it was time to thank the Lord for life, and to ask for some well-placed guidance.

The ranch staff and I had been contacted by thousands of people who had read the book *Hope Rising*. Immediately, a resounding theme began to emerge through this correspondence: "You are living my dream. I never knew it was possible until now… Will you show me how to do the same thing?" Daily, it became an echoing cry for reassurance, encouragement, and help.

*Who am I, Lord, to show them the way?* I thought, in full recognition of all my mistakes and shortcomings. *Sometimes I feel like nothing more than a bare-fisted prize fighter who gets the stuffings beat out of him every other day. Often, I am bruised and bloodied. Perhaps my only real "talent" is just getting back up from all the times that I have been knocked down.*

*For all those looking for direction…Lord, I'm just a simple rancher who loves kids and horses and lives in a nine-acre converted rock pit.* My honest inadequacies were confessed aloud to Sevi and Chloe, my blue-heeler companions, who were hiking with me. As is customary for me, I had found a particularly beautiful viewpoint and began quieting my heart to pray.

There, in the silence, blowing gently through the trees and swirling into my heart, a familiar, peaceful response began to whisper: "You are a simple rancher who loves kids and horses and lives in a nine-acre converted rock pit…why *not* you? You are entangled with the same mistakes and shortcomings as everyone else…why *not* you? You are a small pebble plucked from a stream, and when thrown by My hand, giants in the lives of those around you have fallen; it is not your strength, but Mine…why *not* you?"

Sevi and Chloe, sensing that I had completely stilled, followed suit and curled up nose to stubby tail on randomly blown piles of pine needles. With the wind as my witness and hope as my guide, the lingering resistance that once gripped my heart began to crumble away. In the stillness, I could feel it falling until it dashed against the rocks beneath my feet and shattered into irreparable fragments over the melting snow.

Sometimes clarity happens in the most unlikely places—on a mountaintop, in the shower, in bed before sleep, or driving to complete an errand. My time on the ridge-top enforced within me that sometimes it is our "bruising," our weakness, that is truly the most powerful and honest truth we can share. Perhaps it is enough to encourage others by simply stating, "Friends, here are some of the areas where I have fallen. Let me take your hand and guide you around these perils that…by stepping forward in faith…you will be sure to encounter."

———————+|+———————

The hosting of Crystal Peaks Youth Ranch's first "Information Clinic" was incredible! Because of the ranch's limited size, we thought that between forty to fifty participants would be a good fit. Nearly one hundred people came from twenty-three states and Canada! I felt more like royalty than a rancher, as each came bearing their own irreplaceable gifts of blessing to my heart. Within the first hour of gathering together, most of us agreed that this truly felt more like a *family reunion* than a clinic.

During each of the four days of the clinic, the participants were deluged with every angle of information we could think of that might be of help to them. Together we shared our dreams, laughed at each other's humorous vignettes, worked hard to learn new concepts, ate many meals, and even sang around a fire.

Each unique individual's story seemed to weave seamlessly into the next, all together creating an indescribably beautiful tapestry of selflessness, sacrifice, and love. Rarely have I been surrounded by so many individuals who were so focused and united in their pursuit to become a light in their world, to grow where they were "planted," and to offer hope, love, and healing to those around them...through their *own* sacrifice.

As I lay in bed during those nights of the clinic, I couldn't help but look up through the window at the night sky. The clinic participants were just like this, I thought. Cast against such blackness, they were indeed stars radiating hope through a gloomy void. They were sharing with those around them, literally shining, that hope will continue to provide points of light through even the darkest night, guiding the way until dawn's first rays promise the herald of a new day. There will *always* be a new day.

They moved me, every one of them.

Perhaps what I thought were some of the most interesting parts of the clinic were the "demonstration classes." Sprinkled throughout each day were hands-on demonstrations of how to train your horses, how to train yourselves, how to communicate with kids, how to organize a volunteer program, and how to build a supportive staff, just to name a few.

One demonstration that for me, eleven years of observing has not diminished in the least, was watching the farrier trim hooves. Sue is not only a remarkable woman but a remarkable farrier as well. Because she is such an engaging teacher, I always come away with something new from our time spent together.

Often, Sue relates horse hooves to our personal lives, linking the two by how important it is to stay balanced. What might seem like a minor disparity in the hoof can translate up the horse's leg into real trouble. How true that principle can be in our own lives with things that we might delude ourselves into believing that "it's no big deal" or "it doesn't affect anyone but me." Eventually, if unattended, our personal imbalances will reveal themselves in some pretty unpleasant ways.

Probably what I love most about watching Sue correct, reshape, and balance a hoof is how she handles bruises. As awful and debilitating as they may appear in the sole of a horse's hoof, they can be carefully managed. Of all the times that I have watched my dear friend carve away bruises, I am always amazed at the renewal, the fresh perfection that lies waiting to be revealed just beneath the sight of a painful experience.

As the clinic drew to a close, many expressed their gratitude with emotion, laughter, and quietly revealed dreams. Within the four days of sharing information, I was continually amazed at what precious gems of wisdom were mined by these individuals from what often seemed to me like nothing more than a simple matrix.

One woman, in a rare vignette of silence, shared with me that she had an epiphanal moment during the clinic. I watched her intently as she began to describe her unique experience. She was a slender woman with dark features. As she started to share, I could clearly see that this was going to be costly for her. From the very first few words, she worked hard to control her emotions. In a not-so-steady voice, she recounted how this powerful moment came while watching Sue trim a hoof.

In a strong yet quiet voice, she shared that just recently her own dream—her own life's work—had been crushed. "I used to do something very similar to what you are doing now," she softly said. "Within two days, it was all gone...*everything*. Everything I had worked so hard for, everything I believed in, was taken away in a single moment."

Her gaze seemed to be fixed on the letters I held in my hand. "When I came here, I was so deeply bruised," she continued. "My life felt like it could never be the same again. Perhaps I came to this clinic because I needed to believe that somehow my hurting heart could change into something usable again. Maybe I just needed to see with my own eyes that miracles really do still happen."

Visibly, she softened for a moment before simply stating, "God is so good. Two days ago I stood in a semicircle of about twenty-five people and watched a horse's hoof being trimmed. As Sue scraped the sole, she revealed a large purple bruise. As I studied the bruise, it suddenly occurred to me that I was looking at myself! Yep, that is just like my heart right there...one big, hideous bruise. I found myself staring at it and just feeling overwhelming sorrow.

"But then something remarkable happened," she said, in rising revelation. "Sue picked up her hoof knife and began to carefully cut into the bruised area. She explained that as awful as a bruise can look and feel…*time always proves what is true*. 'A bruise needs to be *absorbed*,' Sue clarified. 'After the hoof grows out away from the once damaged vessels, the dead tissue needs to be removed.'

"And then with two expertly placed cuts from her hoof knife…the horrible bruise that at one time had caused so much pain…was gone…completely *gone!* What lay beneath it was a beautiful, brand-new white hoof! I didn't know until that moment that my heart was going to be just like that hoof."

The woman looked directly at my eyes and beamed, "I realized during that moment that I must *absorb* and learn from my 'bruise.'"

I fully understood what she was trying to say. Immediately I could think of dozens of times when this principle was true in my life as well. When we are caught in a season of feeling bruised and in pain, it is often difficult at that time to believe we can feel any other way. Pain is crushing, blinding, paralyzing. It is not unlike the venom of a predator, meant only to numb its prey into uselessness. There, in that "feeling useless" place, we have a choice to make. We can decide to stay paralyzed in our pain, or we can decide to take steps toward our healing.

Sometimes within our healing process some "dead flesh" needs to be excised away. Sometimes the knife of the Maker is needed to release us from our "dead spots" that hold us back from an *honest* recovery. This might smart a bit at the time, but what is revealed beneath that deadness is *always* worth the choice.

The woman's eyes gradually began to soften as she took a deep breath before continuing. "Now I understand that the next cutting away of my 'deadness' might be the last release of my pain from this particular 'blow.' Perhaps," she paused for a long breath, "the next swipe of our Lord's knife will reveal a fresh newness within me that wasn't there before."

She began to smile as she realized the wisdom of her own words. "Until now, I never really understood that the most beautiful thing about a bruise...is that they come...and last until they are absorbed...and then they *go*!"

———++———

*Young Wisdom*

David, age 11: "If I could choose between playing my favorite video games for a week straight or going to the ranch...I would always choose the ranch."

# 17

# Horse with Spots
## (Part 1)

Never in all my years of operating the ranch have I ever experienced such severe "buyers remorse." I had just purchased a very short, very chubby Appaloosa mare. Shonee was certainly cute enough within her roly-poly white body that was completely freckled with black spots. Yet the true reason for the sale by her previous owner—of one week—was the mare's nearly complete refusal to turn or stop at her rider's request. Certainly, those are both truly important features for a kid's horse to have!

Nevertheless, there was something about her that spoke to me. Initially, she appealed to me because of her goofy stature. She was not only disproportionately short for her body; she was also incredibly strong.

The first time I saw her, I nearly laughed out loud. Her front legs were separated by a *huge* chest. The gap between her knees was nearly wide enough to park a Volkswagen! Her body was so large and her legs were so short that she looked a bit like a white, freckled minibus with legs!

Oddly enough, it was a combination I had been looking for. As silly as this seemed, her ridiculous conformation, the overall picture of how she was put together, was an important feature in my mind…because most of the disabled kids that we work with are also short and "round." So a sturdy horse that was low to the ground would be the perfect fit for kids who are a bit heavier and unsure of heights.

Even though my "test drive" with her was somewhat disastrous, complete with constant straining to return to the barn, bucking, and my personal favorite—two attempts at a full-blown "run away"—there was still something *special* about this hefty girl that called out to me.

After loading her into the trailer and paying out one thousand dollars for her purchase price, I climbed into my truck and shut the door. I literally had to grip the steering wheel with both hands for a moment…to keep from *slapping myself in the head!* "Girl! What have you just done?!"

Once at the ranch, Shonee, who had been named after the Shoshone Indian Nation, began her metamorphosis. Somehow, certainly not by any of my genius, this little spotted mare methodically chose to change into what I would consider a candidate for the world's greatest kids' horse. In only a few weeks' time, "simply Shonee," miraculously transformied into "Shonee the Wonder Pony!"

She continually proved to everyone that she could do anything. She was patient with little kids, unbalanced kids, frightened kids, noisy kids, bouncing kids…and the same list could be dittoed for adults as well. She loved bareback-riding and simply being wallowed with affection. For kids who were celebrating their birthday at the ranch, she was often chosen as the "painting horse" because she made such an incredible "canvas." There was something wonderful about connecting her dots with bright red, blue, and orange that was of particular delight to our youthful, paint-smeared "artists."

In parades, she was always a favorite. I often wondered if her spots didn't have some sort of magnetic value, because everywhere she went, she seemed to posses a "gravitational pull" on the young at heart of those who surrounded her.

Concerning unpredictable trail situations, she was always as solid as a sunrise. She never really considered spooking or being flustered about anything. She enjoyed carrying a pack saddle because she quickly learned that somewhere amidst all those supplies was a snack waiting just for her. Nothing seemed to ruffle her in the least—traversing a rushing mountain stream, navigating a difficult trail into an alpine meadow, getting tied to a high line at night, or being blanketed, hobbled, or beset by bees or bug spray. Shonee continued to prove daily that whatever shape it took, she simply enjoyed her life. For her, the method, company, or venue of attention wasn't important as long as she was loved. All that really mattered was love.

Of everyone who adored Shonee, perhaps no one could have been more truly devoted than a young, slender girl named Sarah. After several years of riding at the ranch, it appeared that Sarah's heart was slowly being surrounded by "spots." This shy, tow-headed little blond fell hopelessly in love with Shonee the Wonder Pony.

Born with a genetic deficiency in her vision, Sarah began wearing thick, corrective glasses at the age of two. Learning is challenging enough for kids who can see clearly...it is incomprehensively harder for those who cannot. Sarah remembered being asked by an inquisitive peer, "Are you blind? You look so funny in those lined glasses." Her casual yet brave response was, "Nope, these lines are prisms, and they help to exercise my eye muscles so they get stronger." Sarah was never ashamed of the path God chose for her. Even now, she understands that her "uniqueness" has made her more compassionate, tenacious, and thoughtful.

After six years of prismed glasses, eye patches, eye exercises, and vision therapy, Sarah underwent corrective surgery on both of her eyes. While recovering from her operation, she exclaimed in complete wonder to her mother, "Mom, I *never knew* I had freckles!" Through an incredible amount of hard work and perseverance, Sarah currently enjoys nearly perfect vision and wears glasses only to assist her with distance.

At the ranch, Sarah found the balance in friendship that she so earnestly sought. There was no question that in her eyes, that "balance" was named Shonee.

Innocently unaware, each was leading the other by their simple example of what the foundation of true friendship should really be. Sarah never noticed the funny looking way that Shonee was built, and Shonee never noticed that Sarah had any more struggles than any other girl. All they seemed to truly care about was how much each loved the other.

In an effort to keep her spotted friend close to her heart between visits, Sarah's mother had shared with me how Sarah had literally plastered her room with Shonee pictures: Sarah feeding Shonee flowers, Sarah giving Shonee a bath, Sarah cantering on Shonee for the first time, Sarah and Shonee sharing a kiss. Layer by layer, Shonee became the freckled bricks in the rising wall of Sarah's self-confidence.

Watching Sarah and Shonee together was like watching a butterfly and a flower. Together they became a visual example of something all kids and adults should practice. Instead of quickly judging each other for their unique differences, each seemed to understand and embrace those very distinctions for exactly how they were created...as one of a kind. Instead of rejecting those who are different than ourselves, Sarah and Shonee chose strong friendship, each complementing the other, each making the other better...each loving the other exactly how they were.

Every day they were together, each honored the value of the other, proving how truly precious every moment is with those you love. Because in the end, we never know when the next moment...will be the last...

## 18

# Horse with Spots
## (Part 2)

Because there are so many unwanted horses in the world that need help, the ranch usually chooses not to breed any of its acquired mares. But since the ranch already had a pregnant mare, whose foal would be in need of a playmate, Shonee was instantly elected to become the sweet mother to provide that companion.

Although we knew virtually nothing about Shonee's past, her "stretched" conformation and udder clearly spoke to us that she had already given birth to many foals. With great delight, we could only imagine how incredibly cute her previous babies must have been…and certainly how special her next would be.

After choosing the right stallion for our freckled girl, we had to part with her during her breeding process for an entire month. Everyone on the ranch was highly aware of Shonee's absence. Perhaps more than any other horse, Shonee was chosen as the "first ride" by most of our new riders. Those riders subsequently fell in love with her as well, seeking her out every time they came to the ranch. Without a doubt, the void she left could be filled by no other. She was as unique as a thumbprint, and she had left her hoof print on the hearts of many.

Gratefully, within the multilayered activities of the ranch, Shonee's time away passed quickly and she was returned to a cheering assembly of open arms. Now our greatest challenge concerning Shonee would be to wait the nearly eternal eleven months and eleven days to see what kind of spotted foal we would all be greeting.

As fall began to deepen in color and temperature, it brought with it the cool remembrance of another year silently drawing to a close. The breeze over the high desert had turned brisk, calling through the grass and trees like a messenger proclaiming the imminent narrowing of time before white rest falls. For this particular year, the chill on the back of my neck translated into one thing...book deadline.

I had been asked by Multnomah Publishers to write a "follow up" to my first book, *Hope Rising*. Since the ranch had blossomed into more than a full-time job, the only season that I could endeavor to actually sit and write was deep winter. Even then, many of the ranch staff must not only complete their own jobs but also help shoulder parts of mine to clear a "time path" for me to write.

With my last major speaking engagement of the year complete, Troy and I loaded up our camper and drove to southeastern Oregon. Because of its incredible desolation, it is truly one of my favorite places on earth. I have an extremely public life for which I am very thankful. Yet I am fully aware that one of the major reasons I can tolerate the constant time compression is because of the efforts Troy and I make to maintain some "solitary" time. Having learned from my own failures, I have a deep understanding that a person cannot give...what they do not have.

It is important to understand that as humans, we are finite.

We really *do* have limitations that even the best of intentions cannot supersede. We really *don't* have infinite amounts of any emotion that we wish to share. Therefore, we must be mindful to do our best to "fill the storehouse" with all that we have expended. This "refilling" process can take on as many different shapes as there are people who give. The truly important thing is not what venue we choose to recharge our hearts through… but simply that we do recharge them.

What I love most about southeastern Oregon is that it is *remote*. When the nearest "town" is an hour away and bursting with a population of seven…*quiet* is one of many words that truly define this unique place. I also appreciate that more often than not, the road beneath you will be dirt, and that it leads to neighbors who are not the two-legged type but the four. You never know if you will be meeting heavy mule deer, scattered herds of antelope, burly big-horned sheep, wild horses, bobcat, or even the occasional mountain lion.

Few things fill my heart more than being in the deep wilderness. Little else inspires me with the same vitality as adventuring through the wild places in the morning and then returning back to base camp to work the rest of the day.

Such was this day. Troy was hiking on his own, and my friends Sue and Wayne, who had joined us in the desert, were a good distance away in town, visiting two of the seven folks there. It had snowed hard the night before, and the high, nearly treeless desert had been transformed into what looked more like a vast and flawless tablecloth. Tumbling down from the 9,000-foot peaks that hung overhead, its white splendor unfolded through every deep canyon and spread out into undulating folds over the foothills until its powdery softness eventually smoothed flat over the immense plains. I am convinced that, when surrounded by such immeasurable beauty…even a *stone* could write..

Our camp was suspended on a small bench between the valley floor and the mountains that loomed above. I had been working for many hours when I heard a sound as familiar as a friend's voice—the diesel engine of Sue's truck approaching. "Odd," I thought, since they were not planning to return until dark. As her truck growled up the last incline, I started moving my work to the side so I could step out and greet her. Before I could even open the camper door…she began calling me from outside.

I couldn't reach the door fast enough…*something was wrong*.

Her anxious expression confirmed the fear that was rising within my heart. "Is your cell phone on?" she asked with great tension.

"Uh, no…it doesn't work out here," I answered in a voice that trailed into near silence.

Sue drew in a tight breath, hesitated, and cautiously proceeded. "Apparently your vet has been trying to reach you all morning. Kim…there has been a tragedy at the ranch…"

In the seconds before she continued, endless scenarios of pain and disaster began crashing into my heart like house-sized boulders. I felt as if I was virtually being buried alive beneath an emotional avalanche of all the possibilities of what could be wrong. I could feel the naked pain within Sue's voice as she spoke. *Tragedy at the ranch.* The words reverberated within my chest like a terrifying echo…

Even here, in this remote refuge for my heart…catastrophe had followed my tracks like a predator…and struck.

"Shonee is with the vet. It's bad…they need you to…to…to give the…okay…to put her down."

A myriad of questions immediately log-jammed within my brain. As I fought to untangle them, Sue handed me her phone and said with her eyes, "Mine works…make the call…"

In moments I was speaking to Darrin, who was not only a trusted friend but one of our veterinarians as well. I hardly recognized his gravelly voice…his easygoing tone was gone. What I heard sounded more like a bow string, low and taunt, stretched to near breaking. I could feel my throat closing with the revelation that whatever was going to come out of his mouth was irrelevant…I understood my friend well enough to realize that he already knew…it was over.

Just the tone of his voice…made me want to throw up. Darrin proceeded to recount in gut-wrenching detail how Shonee came into the clinic for a routine pregnancy exam. The purpose of such an exam is to determine if the mare is pregnant so appropriate follow-up measures can be immediately initiated. Understandably, this is valid information, because special vaccinations need to be administered to help prevent the mare from contracting viruses that could cause her to spontaneously abort her foal.

Somehow, during the completely standard rectal ultrasound exam, her rectum was torn. Although such tears are extremely rare, they can occur in isolated cases. Darrin explained that it was a ventral tear…meaning that it was along the bottom of her rectum. Waste materials were leaking into her belly cavity. In a matter of hours she would be septic, and no antibiotic on earth could stop the ensuing infection.

Even though Darrin was not the vet who had performed the procedure, because of our friendship he had taken over the case and was caring for Shonee as if she were his own. Just to be sure…and perhaps a bit for my own heart…Darrin elected to wait a few hours, draw fluids from her belly cavity, and let the results of that test tell us what needed to happen next...

Chris, the overseer of our horse program and the person who, at my request, took Shonee in for her exam, witnessed the entire tragedy. She knew what was about to transpire. With great strength, wisdom, and compassion, she chose to use the extra minutes to bring a few of the older kids from the ranch into the clinic to give as much love and comfort as they could... and to say good-bye.

After a heavy sigh, I switched off the phone. Together, Sue and I knelt on the hillside...and prayed for our little horse with spots.

To ease my breaking heart, I hiked until dark.

When I returned...as I opened the camper door, one look at Troy's ashen face confirmed what I already knew to be true: Shonee...my precious little horse...was dead.

Like a mother grieving for a child lost, I sobbed openly against my husband's chest. In a voice that only God could hear...I let my anguish fall. *Oh Shonee...oh Shonee...not my precious Shonee...Shoneeeeeeee...SHONEEEEEEEE...*

Time and space ceased to exist...all that was real was the crushing grief that consumed my heart.

*Lord, this is so wrong. She was a healthy horse this morning... she left the ranch...and never got to come home. She never got to say good-bye to her family. She was fine...and now she's dead. Where is Your purpose in this? She was the cornerstone of such goodness... such love...how can this be better? How can this be right?*

My anguish continued to gush out in wave after wave of racking, mournful tears. Eventually, my exhausted heart poured out across the flood plains of tearless realization that nothing would ever be the same...except the bedrock of truth within my heart: God is still in control.

No matter how out-of-control my perspective might be, I can rest on what I *know* is true; it has been true my whole life, proven over and over: God *is* in control.

Slowly, my grief-tattered heart turned from questioning… to resting. *I trust you, Lord…I trust You…even though it doesn't make sense…I trust You.*

Returning home to the ranch was difficult. While driving up the driveway, I scanned the herd as I always do. Shonee's absence was gaping. Once the chores were done and everyone had left for the day…I went and just hung on the main corral gate…and cried…mourning the fact that my beloved Shonee would never pass through this gate again.

When I was able, I pulled my heart back together and summoned the courage to call my friend Lynai…the mother of little Sarah.

After a painful recounting punctuated with many tears, Lynai confirmed that her little girl's tender heart was completely obliterated. "She told me she never wants to come to the ranch again. It would be too painful…because there will never be another Shonee. She will never be able to love another horse like her Shonee Girl."

Gratefully, time always proves what is true. In this case, time proved that the heart of a child, when handled with care, is a very resilient thing.

With careful consideration, little Sarah decided that she would try one more time to come to the ranch. She chose to come on the last day of the year that the ranch would be open for riding. Just in case things didn't go well, she could leave and have no reason to ever come back.

Sarah worked with Chris, who was masterful in choosing a young horse that was still in training and had yet to be ridden by a child. Sarah had felt so honored to be the "first kid" to ride Phoenix. Under Chris's gentle instruction, Sarah's time on the ranch was a successful relief to all, especially after Sarah gave Phoenix a bath and led her into the arena for a roll. Phoenix didn't quite understand what Sarah wanted her to do…so I suggested that she get down in the sand and *show* her! True to form, Sarah rolled like a little champion and hoorayed in triumph when Phoenix finally understood and dropping into the sand, rolled with her.

Chris built the bridge…and Sarah *chose* to cross.

When the day was all but over, I looked for Sarah to give her a hug of support and congratulate her on her victorious ride…and roll. After a bit of searching, I found my little friend curled up on a fence rail by the main corral gate. Stepping through the fence poles, I sat down beside her. Even though her tiny face was turned away, it was clear that she was crying.

Certainly, it is our actions that prove what is true. No words were going to soften the pain for either of us. Our actions reflect what is truly inside our hearts. So there on the fence, shoulder to shoulder, hand in hand and heart to heart…we wept.

Finally, when her tears were spent, she slowly moved her head backward and looked up into my face. Although she said nothing, her expression was questioning.

*Lord, it is time to rebuild her foundation. Please help her to understand…and trust*, I prayed before I began to speak. "Shonee was one of the greatest horses that ever lived. She made us all better just by being our friend. Without her, the ranch will never be the same. It will be *different*. Shonee knew that you loved her every day of her life, even to her last minutes. She was loved all the way to heaven's gate. Sarah…I have something that I need to share with you…"

I took a deep breath and continued to silently pray for wisdom.

"Sarah, love is a very powerful thing…especially the *pure* love of a little girl. Your love, Sarah, is a precious gift to those you choose to give it to…it changes them from the inside out. Being loved changes us all. Honey, your special love…is special indeed. I think that your Shonee Girl was completely *full* of your love—enough to last a whole entire lifetime. Maybe…just maybe…it is time for another hurting horse to be filled up…to have their life changed by your special love. Do you think that it's possible?" I asked in a small voice as I held her upward gaze.

Magnified by her glasses, her round eyes were so big they looked more like deep blue moons. I don't know if it was their size or depth or the fact that they were shimmering with tears, but in that moment Sarah's eyes seemed to be penetrating my very soul.

Momentarily she glanced to the side as she contemplated the new idea that I had just presented: Could there be another horse that needed her special love? The wheels of possibility churned within her. When she seemed to have reached a conclusion, she turned back to me and, without a word, solemnly nodded.

As Shonee "ran on ahead"…perhaps another was trailing behind…another who was lagging back in brokenness…another who was in great need of the love of a little blond girl with thick glasses.

# 19

# Horse with Spots
## (Part 3)

The first heavy snows of winter were beginning to fall, and with it came an unusually heavy amount of folks who were wishing to donate horses to our ranch. Since the ranch is located on only nine *tiny* acres…our corrals "runneth over" with our own herd of twenty-five to thirty horses. Because not every horse that the ranch rescues is destined to be suitable for children, horses that are not a "fit" for our program are adopted out into appropriate homes…occasionally making room for others to come in.

While walking around the snow-laden "block"—which, where I live, is about four miles—Chris and I were catching up on all that had transpired since our last time together. Conversation flowed easily between us as we carefully navigated the snow and ice. When we turned the final corner toward home, Chris suddenly burst out, "Oh my gosh! *Now* I remember what I was going to tell you. Remember the folks from Washington who bought that little gelding for their daughter? They sent more information yesterday. You're not going to believe this…"

Once Chris had revived my leaky memory, she launched into the next chapter of information. A young mother wished to buy a small horse for her six-year-old daughter so they could trail-ride together. After finding what appeared to be a suitable horse—small, quiet, slow, uncomplicated, and patient—they brought the little gelding home and quickly realized that his "quiet" temperament was attributed to the fact that he had been drugged! The small gelding "awoke" into a very frightened, nervous, head-shy little man who had all the markers of a horse who had been violently battered.

Even though this little horse was obviously not the right one for their family, the mother could not, would not return him to the home where his abuse was perpetrated. Instead she kept him for nearly three years and sheltered him as her own, daily leading him down the path of kindness, trust, and love. All the while, she knew that this special tiny gelding had come into her life for a reason, for a purpose as yet…unknown.

The generous mother of two inadvertently became the mother of three. Within the years the little horse was in her company, she lived such an example of love and compassion that his life was changed forever because of it. The gelding's fright was replaced by peace, his nervousness by calm, his fear of being touched by loving to be touched. She had built the bridge…and he chose to cross it.

The gentle mother, realizing that her adopted "son" was now ready for his born destiny, called our ranch for advice about perhaps placing him with us or a trusted family.

"And that's not even the amazing part of the story," Chris beamed. "*You have to see this,*" she continued, as she nearly led me by the hand into the bunkhouse toward the computer. Within a large stack, she quickly located a printed e-mail with a picture. Turning around, she held it up at head-level, not far from my face, and said, "Who does *this* look like?"

Leaning toward the picture, I squinted as I absently took it from her hand. *Oh Dear Lord…what are You doing to my heart?* I could feel my eyes beginning to flood as the picture came into sharp focus. The best I could do was raise my hand over my mouth for a moment and wait for my throat to relax. I looked up at Chris and quietly stated what she already knew was true.

"He looks like…Shonee."

Other than a few minor differences, the small gelding in the picture looked like a male version of our Shonee. Certainly, he could easily pass for her little brother. He was a white Pony of America…covered in little black spots. His name was Gideon. "The little horse that could," I thought to myself.

As usual, my heart ran far ahead of my brain, immediately making plans of how we could move him to the ranch. *Whoa, girl*, began to rise out of what was left of my reason. *The ranch is full…there is no space available for him to come.* In what was starting to feel like a "slug fest," my heart countered back with my personal "poster child" of truth: "Yeah, but you *know* that if God is in it…*He* will provide for it!"

For an adult with dyslexic and ADHD tendencies, it is not uncommon for me to feel pulled apart by internal conversations. *Okay, okay: Heart and head…go to your separate corners! Truth has spoken. If it is God's wish that Gideon comes to the ranch…a space will become available for him. It is not wise to rush headlong into what we think we want; allow God's wisdom to prove what is true. Head…do you agree? "Yes." Heart…do you agree? "Yup." All right then, now let's get back on the tracks and start pulling together…* With my mini-uprising put down, it was time to rest in what I knew was always true.

I had kept Lynai, Sarah's mother, current on all the recent possibilities. Only days later she shared with me through an e-mail a very poignant conversation that she had just had with her little girl:

"Kim, since you told me about Gideon, I have been talking to God about Sarah's heart and her acceptance of him. This morning Sarah cuddled up beside me and asked if I thought she could ever love a horse again. 'Absolutely! We don't just love one person, we love many people, each held in a special place in our hearts.' Sarah thought about that for a moment before she quietly said, 'Momma, I think that I'm ready to love a horse again...but not just any horse...I need a horse with spots...like Shonee...that way her memory will always be with me. Are there any other horses like her? Do you think that Kim will ever find another like my Shonee?"

As it is within the heart of a father...truly, the very foundations of heaven must quake with adoration...when little girls pray.

A week and a half later...a space became available...Gideon was on his way.

It was only days before Christmas, and the Pacific Northwest was buried beneath a heavy snowfall. For several weeks the temperature barely reached into the low teens. No one anticipated that on the day Gideon was scheduled to arrive, the area would be overwhelmed by a "Pineapple Express"—unusually warm, tropical winds would be suddenly diverted into the region on a radically shifted jet stream. The ensuing meltdown, combined with freezing rain, caused some of the worst travel conditions in recent history. The roads were so treacherous that travel of any kind, even a short distance, was unwise. In such perilous conditions, to try and imagine traveling several hundred miles while pulling a horse trailer was out of the question. Gideon would have to wait for another day, perhaps even another season.

The following morning dawned with even warmer temperatures. Instead of bundling up for five-degree weather, I was shedding layers for forty-five degrees and climbing! In the few hours it took me to drive to town, work out with a friend, and drive home, the roads were not only breaking up nicely, they were becoming downright drivable.

While rounding the last bend in the road before the ranch, I noticed a truck and trailer pull into the driveway just ahead of me. *You've got to be kidding!* I thought, as my mouth fell open. Yesterday I could barely *walk* on the ranch, never mind driving a few hundred miles to reach it. I was completely incredulous as I realized that little Gideon had arrived.

After excited introductions and a hasty call to Lynai, a wonderful chain reaction was now unfolding. Gideon was here, he was kind and far more beautiful than any photograph could have ever captured...and little Sarah was on her way.

My new friends who brought Gideon to us assured me that nearly their entire trip down was on dry pavement. The weather on the west side of the Cascade Divide had been much warmer for much longer. Apparently, only the last thirty miles were a bit tenuous. I was greatly relieved to hear that they did not imperil themselves or their precious gift. Not wishing to drive over the pass during the evening freeze, my friends wisely chose to head back over the mountains while the sun was at its highest. After many hugs and a few tears, they waved good-bye and left nearly as quickly as they came.

I had not yet turned around to walk up the driveway when Lynai and Sarah arrived. "Hey, little cowgirl!" I hailed to Sarah as she rounded the back of their car and hugged me tightly. "I am so glad that you are here. This little horse really needs you," I continued. Sarah's mouth was smiling, but her eyes were questioning. We both looked at Lynai. "She doesn't know *anything*," she said with a broad grin.

"Hmmm…" I bent down until I was resting my hands on the top of my knees, nearly eye to eye with my small friend. In my mind, it was vitally important that she understand why I had invited her to come to the ranch. "Sarah, do you remember when we sat on the fence together and I shared with you how incredibly special your love is? How much it changes those you share it with?"

Immediately she recognized by my posture that this was a significant moment. Her uniquely magnified eyes were as large as quarters as she blinked up at me. Her mouth parted open, but instead of using words, she nodded somberly.

I continued. "A horse has just come to the ranch. He is a very extraordinary, small gelding who has traveled from far away to this new home. Sometimes that is scary. Being afraid is not what we wish for anyone on the ranch…that's why you are here…I need your special love to help this little horse know that there is no need for him to be afraid because he is not alone…he's going to be okay…he's going to be loved. Do you think you can help me with that?"

Once again, with the innocence of a child, she nodded her head and added a little "Uh-huh."

That very attitude is one of the things I love most about kids. *"Hey, little kid, do you want to help save the world?"* *"Sure!"* Because they don't doubt that they can…they just do!

Hand in hand, we walked up the long driveway that leads to the ranch common yard. Gideon was in paddock number one, which is directly behind the barn. She could not see him as we walked toward his paddock. It wasn't until we walked all the way into his corral that she saw a white pony with a long white mane and tail, standing in deep white snow. Truly, all that was missing was the shaft of light from heaven. There he stood, looking very much like a four-legged angel.

Sarah was struck silent.

I opened the gate for both Sarah and her mom to pass through. Arm in arm, mother and daughter walked on together. As they drew near to Gideon, Sarah turned her face into her mother's side. Without a sound…she began to cry.

I walked ahead and began to rub the small horse's neck. I looked back at Sarah. I could only imagine what was happening inside her heart. Finally, I simply nodded my head toward Gideon, indicating that I wanted her to come and join me.

She approached him very slowly, wordlessly, as if he was a dream.

I watched as only the tips of her fingers made hesitant contact with his white winter coat. Instead of vanishing, he turned slightly to look at her…and she looked back. I moved to the opposite side of Gideon so they could clearly see each other.

Sarah allowed her finger tips to spread slowly apart until the palm of her hand was resting flat against his back. Then she raised her other hand and repeated nearly the same process.

Completely lost in her own thoughts, she silently began to run her hands over his back, neck, and face. Mesmerized, her expression revealed that all creation had slipped away...there was left only a little blond girl...loving a little horse with spots.

After a moment, I returned with a halter. Together, we led Gideon through the rapidly melting snow toward the hitching post for his first grooming session at the ranch. His exceptionally heavy mane and tail, proof of his pony heritage, were tinged a vague reddish color, evidence of a life lived on clay. Sarah and I agreed that if it was a little warmer, we would have soapy buckets out in no time, restoring his glory to a shiny white. We both laughed at how the black hair that made up his spots, for some unknown reason, stood straight up. Therefore, his black spots were slightly raised above his white body, making him look like a giant domino...in reverse.

Lynai was well-prepared and brought a large bag of carrots. Any uncertainty Gideon might have had about being in a new home was quickly overwhelmed by his passion for snacks. In no time his mouth was so full that the excess carrot juice combined with his saliva to make a brilliant orange foam. There was so much froth that the surplus drooled out of his mouth and onto the snow beneath him.

I glanced at Sarah. She looked happy.

Gideon, still chewing away, held his head low, his eyes half-mast. He was happy too.

With the evening feeding complete and Gideon settled back in his temporary corral, I returned from putting a few feed pans away to find Sarah sitting on the rail fence about ten feet from our new pony's head. Even though he was casually munching hay, they were positioned face to face. She was sitting very still...just watching him...only him. I quietly joined her mother who was sitting on a separate section of fencing about thirty yards away.

Like a sentry waiting for dawn, Sarah watched in complete silence for more than twenty minutes…nearly a lifetime for a kid. In the stillness, I could only wonder…and trust…that her heart was being visited by resolution, restoration, and rekindling.

My mind drifted toward the truth that no horse can ever replace another. I began to wonder if this whole event was just a bit too overwhelming for Sarah. Was it too much, or too soon, to encourage her forward out of her grief? Perhaps what initially seemed like such a good idea really wasn't; it was only my hope to ease her sadness.

My thoughts were cut short as Sarah began to move.

She slipped off the railing. As hushed and slow as the moon travels across the sky, she silently moved to his side. Standing with her back toward us, I could see she was resting her right hand on his withers while rubbing his neck with her left. Gradually her right elbow crossed over his back as she leaned against him. Slowly her small neck begin to flag as her head lowered until it rested on top of Gideon's neck.

Afternoon shadows were getting longer. As the sun was sinking…a heart was rising.

Sarah's hands were imitating the sun and moon—one was going down and the other was going up. One hand reached over Gideon's neck while one hand reached under. Meeting somewhere on the other side, they came together to complete the circle…a circle that looked very much like an embrace… the kind saved only for deep, dear friends.

Joining the retiring sun as a witness, I watched Sarah's embrace linger for long moments.

When it seemed appropriate, I left my perch on the fence

and quietly filled the vacancy that she had just left. Now, only a few feet away from Sarah and her new friend, I smiled at her…and she smiled back.

"What do you think?" I asked as long shadows began to combine.

"He's really nice," she said through a small grin.

Apparently, only after Sarah felt that Gideon had been thoroughly loved, she joined me back on the fence. Being the snuggle-bug that she is, with practiced proficiency she nestled in under my arm.

Although I'm not sure why, I find that watching horses graze is one of the most peaceful things a weary soul can do at the end of the day. Perhaps this is because it embodies pure contentment…in the simplicity of life.

Looking down at Sarah, I wanted to validate what I thought she might be thinking. I asked, "Do you think that God answers prayers?"

She looked up at me with a bit of confusion over my random question before answering with a simple "Uh-huh."

I continued, "Do you think that God has answered *your* prayers?"

A little light went on somewhere inside and twinkled out through her eyes as she responded with a big nod and an even bigger "Uh-huh!" True to her prayers…he was a horse with spots.

"Sarah…" she looked back into my face. "Even though he looks like your Shonee Girl…he will never be Shonee. He will be special in a *different* way…he will be Gideon. Your mom was right, we don't just love one horse or one person. Our hearts have the capacity to hold *lots* of love…enough to love many people and many horses. When we lose someone we love, things will never be the same…they will be different. But different doesn't mean bad…it just means that our love has the opportunity to be poured out in another direction. Our love only goes where we choose it to…so we have to *choose* for our love to go forward…otherwise it gets stuck. And then special love isn't special anymore."

I didn't ask Sarah for an answer or a commitment. It was a time to simply share truth with a child.

In the sweet and silent moments that followed, I couldn't help but reflect on all the loss that I, too, have known; my parents, my grandparents, and my friends of both the two-legged and four-legged kind. It occurred to me that love really is a bridge that can cross *any* span of grief…no matter how wide… love builds the bridge…it is we…who must *choose* to cross.

———— ┼┼┼ ————

*Young Wisdom*

Will, age 17, wrote these words:
"Dust into dust…time to reverse the lies…this ranch
is where sorrow endz…and hopes arise."

Cheyenne, age 7, when being led on a horse by
one of the staff: "Can I let go with my hands?…
Can I also let go with my feet?…*Hey Mom…look!…
I'm ridin' with just my cheeks!*"

# 20

# Friendship

As often as I am able, you will find my tracks leading toward the mountains. This love of the high places was instilled within me by my dad. When I was five, he patiently towed me, with my hands tucked into the back pockets of his jeans, up my first mountain. I remember noticing how the whole world seemed to turn into stone. A cold wind kept whipping wild strands from my self-imposed "haircut" across my face.

After climbing up to the very summit, we discovered that someone previously had stacked rocks in a low-walled semi-circle that we snuggled up against for shelter. There we sat, scrunched together, looking down on the entire world below and the entire sky above. My heart was never the same. I was hooked.

Only a few short years later, my parents died. It was not an "accident"…it was a murder-suicide. It was the end of everything I once knew. Fed by shock, bewilderment, and debilitating sorrow, a gaping vortex ripped open before me, and I fell screaming into its black center as my entire life was swallowed whole.

Gone…all of it.

All that I had once loved vanished…forever. *Everything* within my life changed.

My once brilliantly colored world had been stripped down to pure black. Like a blind soul groping through the darkness, I searched for something…anything…that was familiar. I desperately needed a handhold to grip, something to embrace with all my might, to keep from being sucked further down.

Over time, my world of black began to yield dark shades of gray. Gray relaxed into a thousand different colorless fragments. Slowly, light, color, hope began to peer from a distant horizon. It called me to fight…fight for my life.

Armed only with the pliable heart of a child, I started climbing again.

From the day my parents died, the high places continued to call me with a conifer voice. Carried on a fragrant breeze, my soul could hear its silent whispers…the voice of the mountains was stirring within. My driver's license hadn't even cooled in my wallet before I was gone. I drove as fast as the law would allow toward a cherished place called Castle Crags. Through my years of climbing-drought, its granite towers remained a fortress of stone once enjoyed long ago with my dad. Located close to the northern rim of the California border, it remains hallowed ground within my heart to this day.

From that time on, I always envisioned everything that weighed my heart down as being just too heavy to follow me into the mountains. The higher I climbed, the further I distanced myself from all the pain that threatened to destroy my peace of mind. Whether my heartaches waited for my return to the valleys, I did not know. For my focus was riveted on what I knew to be true: In the mountains…I was free.

Still foundational within my heart today, the high places are where I feel the closest to the Lord, where I hear His voice within my heart clearly, where I am restored by His grace from the inside out. Either by skis, hiking boots, horses, snowshoes, or mountaineering crampons, the method really doesn't matter to me as much as just exploring this amazing world. The deeper I go into the wilderness…the better. The longer I get to sleep in my tent…the better. The higher I am in elevation…the better. The longer I get to wear my same dirty shirt…the bet— Okay, my friends might have a different view on that one!

Thankfully, I have been blessed with a handful of women in my life who share a measure of this same passion. Together we have experienced many pack trips into half a dozen different wilderness areas. In varying combinations of women, back-packs, horses, horse packs, skis, and a myriad of gear, each trip has yielded its own irreplaceable moments of intense friend-ship. More often than in all other places combined, it is within these cherished wilderness areas that my close friends—with timing, grace, and respect—are able to share with me perhaps not what I would *like* to hear…but what I *need* to hear. When founded on the bedrock of loving truth, friendship can become the stone by which we, as individuals, are made sharp.

On one such trip, the trailhead of the Marble Mountains wilderness area in Northern California was the gathering place of our group of four women and three horses. Our team was comprised of a farrier named Sue—the trip leader and "map master"; a human and animal chiropractor named Kris, who possesses a truly sparkling smile—she has a diamond imbedded in one of her teeth (no kidding!); plus a horse trainer dubbed "Kate the Great," whose trademark laughter was always the best way to find her in wide open spaces.

Preferring to carry my own backpack, I usually bring up the rear. It is a wonderful vantage point to partake of the com-pany of such fun and capable friends.

After driving down the night before and rising early, we laid out every item we would need for the next week on several large tarps. We began by accounting and carefully condensing our supplies into horse packs called panniers. Each pannier was weighed and reweighed to ensure that they would be exactly equal and ride comfortably balanced on one of the three horses we brought. The panniers contained supplies for ourselves and the horses, with additional food and shelter. The horses would pack all the gear so my friends were free to walk in front of them carrying a lighter day pack.

Once the panniers were loaded on the horses, they were secured with a diamond hitch. After a final check of every knot, with every cinch retightened, my backpack was hoisted into place and we were finally ready to head out into the glorious unknown. With full understanding that most day-hikers do not usually travel more than ten miles a trip, we know that once we pass the five-mile marker into the wilderness, we will see few others. Because our base camp was going to be almost twenty miles in…we were nearly assured that we would not see another human being until we came back out a week later.

After joining hands in a simple prayer of thanksgiving, gratitude, and safety…we set off.

Always researching areas to bring my staff and kids, I took notice of how the trail began by a beautiful yet crushingly cold river. I had filtered water from it the evening before and was astonished at how clumsily numb my hands were by the time I had finished. We were going to vaguely follow the river up through the mountains to one of its main sources, which was a small, alpine lake. For the next several hours we hiked, completely immersed in the ever-changing forest. What started out as majestic oaks and lower-elevation pines slowly transitioned into towering ponderosa that gradually intermixed with soft, deep-green firs and a few richly fragrant incense cedars.

When we finally pulled up for lunch, we discovered that every pack trip—just like every wedding—has its "hitches." Because I had hopscotched up in front of the last horse, no one noticed that a piece of our vital gear had worked its way free of the last horse's pannier and was somewhere behind us. Everyone turned and looked at me and started laughing. "You're currently training for a marathon…a few extra miles will only make you more tough, more leathery!"

"Okay, okay…uncle!" I replied in mock protest. I was more than happy to get out from under my pack.

Because it is not wise to travel alone in the mountains, good-natured Kate joined me. Together we found our errant item of gear lying in the middle of the trail nearly two miles behind us.

Once reunited with the others, we loaded up again and set out to finish what we had started. The trail took an inspiring but heavy upswing. The mighty forest began to shrink in stature with the apparent heavy snow loads of winter. The earlier firs were looking more stunted and began to intertwine with gnarled, high-altitude white pine.

After several hours of stair-stepping up the steep, rocky trail, we began to breathlessly joke about the true meaning of the lyrics to the song "Stairway to Heaven." Finally, the trail crested on an intersecting ridge, and the lake came into view far below on the other side. By the time we reached the timbered shore, darkness was fast approaching.

In nearly fluid harmony, we unloaded, fed, and watered the horses, stretched high-lines to secure them for the night, set up a makeshift kitchen, and started dinner.

The next task at hand was for each individual to pitch her own tent before total darkness. I strapped on my head lamp and, because I am a very light sleeper, began scouting a small distance away from the kitchen and horses. Quickly locating a perfect spot, I kicked aside a few pine cones and bear "piles" and set up what would become my home for the next week.

Once dinner was consumed, we "bear-proofed" all of our food by hoisting it up into the branches overhead. As much as I appreciate the "neighbors," I am a bit saddened when they raid my camp, and I'm downright grumpy when they eat my food!

As quickly as the night fell, so did our eyelids. A black, moonless cape enveloped the mountains in total darkness. After such a full and wonderfully strenuous day, my pillow—which was nothing more than a fleece shirt stuffed with clothing—was calling.

Slowly waking in the early gray light, I could hear the soft rhythm of rain on my tent. *How could we be so lucky*, I thought. Perhaps for most, rain in the wilderness equals a closed-in, abbreviated, soggy trip. As hard-driving as my life is, the pattering sound on the roof of my tent sounds more to me like a mountain lullaby. "Girl, one of your big chores today…is to take a nap!" For those in need…no sweeter words were ever spoken! No radios, cell phones, message boards, sticky notes, paper piles, or lap tops…wet nylon walls never looked so good!

During a bite of breakfast under a suspended tarp with my friends, I couldn't help but ponder how incredible these women really are. They see me at my absolute worst…yet they insist on loving me still, ugliness and all. Truly they are my "balance beam." With incredible stability, they hold me up. During the times when I struggle and flail, they remain strong and stable; always the same…bearing me upon their straight backs until I once again find my center of balance. Beneath a soaking, dark gray sky, I marveled at my friends. *What a remarkable gift*, I thought, as I watched them share hot cereal, stories, and laughter.

After breakfast I took my own advice and went back to my tent. Especially for those whom rest does not come easily, I am completely convinced that one of the greatest privileges known in the entire world is to simply sleep…until you wake up. Manna from heaven could not be as sweet! The wilderness will still be there when you wake up…just waiting to be explored.

For now…hush, tired heart and thirsty earth…pure water is falling from the sky.

The storm broke the following day. Sunlight began to filter down through the tall stand of fir that bordered the rim of the lake where we were camped. All the world sparkled in radiant glory as billions of suspended raindrops hung heavy from every branch, needle, and blade of grass. No human-carved diamond could ever match even a single drop as it hung suspended, casting intricate rainbows from its liquid center, completely free for any eye to behold. Incomprehensible "wealth" sparkled from every surface…as far as the eye could see. Awe-inspired silence followed us as we set out from our sodden, steaming shelters to experience the wonders of the world around us.

That night we indulged our senses even further by carrying our sleeping mats out into a clearing. Finding grassy carpets of earth, we laid down under the night sky. Beneath the wonder of a purple blanket of stars, with "glitter" reflecting in our awe-filled eyes, we contemplated how truly *good* it is to be alive.

As with every adventure I have ever participated in, each day bears its own unique, intrinsic rewards. After several days of much exploration and discovery, it was time to spend a day scouting toward the highest lake we could find...and take a bath. Packing our biodegradable soap, lightweight towels, food, and any clean clothing we had left, everyone set out together to scale the ridge to our north.

We followed a rising trail carved through gray granite formations that looked more like rows of gigantic whale-backs than extrusions of stone. With moderate effort, we finally reached the ridgetop. Unable to find a trail leading to the lake, we counseled with our maps, compasses, and each other until we agreed on the correct direction to hopefully come out where we believed the lake to be.

Our toil and sweat was greatly rewarded when we finally located the lake. As with other extraordinary finds in the wilderness, this lake was a true gem. Grass intermixed with granite lined nearly half of its meandering shore. The other half was divided between a large talus flow that looked as if it had once thundered ominously into the lake, filling its depths with truck-sized boulders, and the rest, which finally soared upward, with equal grandeur, into a dramatic rise towering into what looked like heaven itself.

Before swinging down my pack, I glanced at Sue and pointed with the top of my head in the direction of the mountain. Her returned smile reflected my thoughts exactly: "The bath can wait...because *up we must go!*"

Only moments later we were bushwhacking up its eastern spine. Every switchback rewarded us with a new appreciation of our freshly gained altitude. The view continued to reveal itself like flood-waters receding from a precious treasure. Every time we raised our chins, we realized how much "richer" we had just become.

At one point during our journey upward, Sue and I scaled through a region of rock that was heavily laden with what looked like silica. From pebbles to boulders, all the rocks were shimmering with enormous streaks of silver glitter. Virtually every stone beheld its own work of art. For over thirty minutes we carefully picked up one masterpiece after another, handing them back and forth in complete wonder. Truly at a loss for words to describe the astounding beauty we held in our hands, we always exclaimed something completely insignificant like "Wow! Look at this one…here's another…check this out."

Together we felt as if we had discovered a lost and priceless treasure. Looking back…in this age of superficiality…I realize that we actually had.

As we rounded up to the summit, I took a deep breath as I once again realized that it is here, within these forgotten fortresses of stone, that my heart leans into the wind and begins to soar.

I have learned that if friendship is my kite, it is the winds of the wilderness that draw it upward toward heaven.

Looking down upon the lake far below us, I noticed that the surface of the water was moving…as I have never in my life seen before. I was completely fascinated. It appeared as a brilliant, living thing. Lit by the blazing sun behind us, downdrafts of wind ruffled the lake into patterns that looked very much like wing strokes from a giant bird. As the wind blew, swirling the water in nearly equal radiating patterns, the sun reflected back this remarkable design in a myriad of golden, gleaming prisms. Though my head could almost explain it, my eyes simply marveled in awe at the astounding beauty that filled them.

I couldn't look away. With full understanding that I cannot actually *see* the wind, I can really see only the *evidence* of its existence—I was reminded that faith, like wind, is invisible...but what it moves is not.

At first glance, the surface of the lake appeared to be reflecting only what my mortal eyes could see. Moving in brilliant honey-colored sparkles was a presence skirting over the surface of the water, spinning in every speed and direction, mirroring the shape of repeated unison wing-beats. Yet with the eyes of my imagination, I smiled with the realization that these amazing patterns looked very much like the joyful down-strokes of angel wings as they danced over the waters.

*Dear Lord...how could heaven be any more beautiful than this?* I wondered within my heart. No palace walls or gilded thrones created by the hands of men throughout all of history...none... not *one*...could compare to the glory of sitting in this windwashed place of stone.

While trying to comprehend the enormous splendor stretching around us, Sue reached silently for my hand. (Having now become an unspoken pact between us, we both agree that there is no better place to thank the Maker, than on top of what He has made.) As real, true and immoveable as the stone we sat upon, was the friendship that bound our hearts together. Thankful to once again view such glory, hand in hand, we prayed together. Each of us asking God to show us how to better shoulder, mirror, and encourage the other. Each giving thanks for another moment of life.

Steeping in the moment, I could not have been any more full. It is here, in times like these, that my heart unfurls like a flag, whipping over all creation...while held secure by the roots of pure friendship.

We need friends...all of us. No person or creature can

survive alone. Nor was any person or creature meant to. Real friendship does more than just make us feel better; truly, it makes *us* better. True friendship is strong, purposeful, honest, compassionate, and steadfast. A real friend gently reveals our weakness, while cheering for every step toward our newfound strength.

It holds us up when we are weak.

For me, it is within the example of what has been "made" that I can clearly see the Maker's purpose. If I could see His peace…it must look like these high lakes. If I could see His power…it must look like these mountains. If I could see His faithfulness… it must look like this sunset. If I could see His friendship…it must look like these forests. Perhaps it's not coincidental that the survival of the tallest trees on earth comes from their reliance on the depth of true friendship.

Because of their immense height and remarkably shallow root system, redwood trees should be very susceptible to high wind. Yet they rarely blow down because they practice something truly amazing. Even though they have very superficial roots, they are still free to grow into towering giants because of one simple thing: Redwoods hold each other up.

Initially, it may not look like much support at all when we gaze up into these majestic forests and see these trees only casually touching. What we cannot see is that beneath our feet, few other trees on earth interlock their roots with more tenacity than redwoods. Therefore a redwood tree cannot survive long by itself. It is when they stand together…allowing their intrinsic individuality to weave seamlessly one into the other…that redwoods are truly strong.

When our roots…and hearts…are intertwined together like

the redwoods, we can hold each other up in strength, together standing firm against the winds of adversity.

We need each other. We need to reach out to those around us who are being buffeted by the wind. By choosing to send our love deep into the hearts of those we call friends…our own heart is stabilized, embraced, and nurtured. It doesn't just happen…it is a choice to send out our roots.

It is God who created roots; it is ultimately we…who must choose to use them.

# 21

# Hannah's Legacy

As if inspired to dance to the music blaring from the stereo, strands of long blond hair whipped free from Hannah's ponytail and danced in the wind that poured through her convertible Mustang. The car was a "dream come true," a treasured surprise given to Hannah by her father.

Occupying the seat next to her, with mouth open and tongue wagging, sat another treasure, her truest companion—Halen Van Hannah, her Doberman Pinscher. All who knew them understood that wherever Hannah went, Halen went.

At eighteen, Hannah Dunn's life was as carefree as the classic rock that she sang along to. Balancing on the summit of her golden high school years, she chose to be many things—loving daughter, friend, honor student, horseman, cheerleader, track athlete, and fisherman. Like any teenager, she loved her family, friends, horses, the outdoors, and cruising behind her dad on his Harley.

Hannah was also completely zealous about putting the needs of others before her own. She was determined, strong, joyful, balanced, fearless, and compassionate. Giving of herself through volunteerism was for her was as natural as breathing. Hannah could regularly be found donating her time to the local police department and the Red Cross. In her mind there was no such thing as a stranger; everyone deserved her attention because everyone deserved to feel liked and special.

It would be impossible to know Hannah apart from her most endearing trademark—her "quick draw" smile and the laughter that always followed. No matter what circumstance she found herself in, she always sought the brighter side and encouraged her peers to do the same.

As a young, natural leader, Hannah taught those around her to overcome their fear. Justice flowed as freely within her chest as her own blood. Like a lioness, she was fierce in her protection of the weak. She regularly used her voice to speak up for those who had none, and she sought to be an advocate for those in need.

Hannah's youth never stopped her from striving for what she believed in—*doing what she knew was right*. At her school, she made a point to reach out to what most would consider the "fringe" kids, those who did not easily fit in with others. One afternoon, she shared with her mother how she had befriended two new girls: "Mom, you know what they told me today? They said, 'We couldn't believe that you would actually *want* to be our friend. *Nobody* as beautiful as you *wants* to be friends with girls like us.'" Hannah continued to recount how happy she was that these girls trusted her enough to lean against her as their own self-confidence took root.

---

"One of our horses has just died…can you help us?"

The urgent plea came from a woman who had owned two horses but had recently lost one. She explained how the horse had died by intentional poisoning from an unknown soul who clearly wished to have fewer horses in the neighborhood.

"Seven horses in our local area have already died," she went on to clarify. "My girls and I do not wish to be without our remaining horse, but we cannot bear losing her as well, especially in this cruel way. It is our understanding that the poisonings are happening at night, so the only way we can fully protect our remaining horse is by keeping her in our garage."

As soon as we were able, Chris and I made the forty-mile trip to check out this sad situation. All we knew about the remaining horse was that she was a mottled gray, small, pony-ish five-year-old from the Warm Springs Indian Reservation. We were told that since the sudden death of her best friend, the little mare was reduced to uncharacteristic fear, spookiness, and deep sorrow over the loss of her soul mate. We were also made aware that the neighboring colt—with whom she shared a fence, and who was also a close friend—had died from poisoning as well.

Upon our arrival, the extremely kind woman who had asked for our help led us out into their nearly empty corral. During the daylight hours, they were turning the little horse out for some fresh air.

When we first saw the gray mare, she was lying down. "That's no pony," I thought, as we quietly approached her. Apparently napping, she was a bit startled by the visitors and quickly rose to her feet…huge feet! It was immediately clear that this "little" mustang was at least fourteen hands, with the bone structure and wavy mane and tail often characteristic of a draft-crossed breed.

She turned to look at us with the large, slightly crowned head of her apparently massive ancestors.

Her owner laughed a little and stated how a couple had recently come to purchase this mare…until they saw her head. In not so careful terms, the potential buyers made it known that this horse was far too "unlovely" for them to consider purchasing.

I looked at her with complete fascination and curiosity. In my eyes, she was not homely in the least. I felt instead that she possessed a strangely unique, powerful beauty that one might associate with a small horse of war. In her own right…she was stunning.

Together Chris and I carefully evaluated the mare. As we customarily do on the drive home, we discussed everything that we saw and felt while observing the small, gray girl. In effective unison, we both agreed—we were completely smitten with this sweet horse and would bring her home as quickly as we could make a space for her on the ranch.

In the time before we brought the mare home, I privately contemplated what her future might become with us.

Since the beginning of the ranch, it has been customary to rename nearly all the horses that have come up our hill. I have always felt that a name is a title that they will hear often, a banner of honor under which they will live. Amongst our herd, almost every horse's name has a special meaning to each individual, often something to be aspired toward.

The gray mare would certainly need a new name because the one she had was already in use by one of the equine "pillars" of the ranch. Even though I contemplated at length an appropriate name for her, and listened to many wonderful suggestions…there was nothing that just seemed to fit.

So often as it is in this walk of faith, we usually do not clearly see the next step until it is virtually under our feet. It wasn't until the day that we brought the gray mare home…that something astonishing, remarkable, and unspeakable happened.

————+|+————

While working in the office, Troy was just starting to wade through his e-mail messages when one title caught his eye. It simply read "For Hannah."

The e-mail began by introducing a young woman named Hannah Dunn. She was a senior from Highland High School in Indiana, and for those who knew her best, she was a country girl to the core. Although she was an excellent student, she rarely read books for pleasure, and even then was not easily impressed. Apparently she had recently read the book *Hope Rising* and was so deeply stirred and inspired by its message that she was moved to emotion. Upon finishing it, she purposefully determined that she would be moved not only to tears…but also to *action*.

Hannah realized that there were basically two ways that she could help. She understood that she could choose whether to "give a man a fish or teach a man how to fish." In her mind, that meant that one option was to send help to Crystal Peaks Youth Ranch directly. Or…after reading *Hope Rising,* she clearly saw and understood that the fun she had been having all along in her backyard with her personal horse "Big John" and friends was perhaps helping them even more than she realized. A greater purpose galvanized within her heart to reach out to even more around her who might need this benefit.

In typical Hannah style…she chose to do both.

With all the money she had earned, Hannah bought as many items for the ranch as she could. While sitting together with her mother at the table, Hannah packaged her gifts for mailing and shared how she believed that her life would never be the same: "Mom, even though I have helped others and 'officially' volunteered, I don't think that I realized just how simple it is to be a 'living volunteer'...to reach out to others all the time...with *whatever* you have."

Hannah conveyed how much she loved horses, running, cheerleading, camping, sleeping in the barn...how much she loved them mostly for *her*...for all the fun and happiness that they had given just her. She understood that although all these things involved other girls, she really never thought before how completely *easy* it would be to shift her focus from how these things benefited only herself...to how she could allow them to benefit those who might need her friendship, support, and encouragement.

Hannah's mother was so moved by her daughter's selfless realization that she reached across the table and pulled her into a firm hug.

The e-mail message went on to recount a school morning not long afterward that began in a typical way. Hannah came down the stairs and spent some time just talking with her mom. When it was time to go, she and her mother hugged each other strongly, as they always did. During their embrace, her mother whispered, "I love you" into her daughter's ear and Hannah repeated it back into her mother's ear before letting go. Together they walked to the backdoor where her mother said, "Have a good day..." As Hannah walked out to her car, she called back, "Okay." Her mother closed the back door and watched her girl drive away toward another day of high school.

Forty-five minutes later, the stillness of the morning was broken by a sharp knock on the front door. Hannah's father opened it to find a county policeman waiting for him. In a soft voice he reported that Hannah had been involved in a car accident and had been rushed to the hospital.

At 7:12 a.m., on February 24...Hannah died.

---

It was the end of a long day and I had just come up the hill from the ranch and into my office. Only moments behind me, I heard the familiar sounds of Troy coming up the steps into our home. Twenty-five years of marriage has taught me many things about my husband; immediately I could hear that his steps were "heavy." I knew that either he was exhausted...or something very hard had happened.

The sounds coming from the other room were as familiar to me as my own heartbeat. It was easy to visualize him pulling off his boots and throwing his jacket, hat, and gloves into the old rocking chair as he walked into the kitchen.

Rising from my chair, I walked to the doorway of my office and just watched him for a moment. It was heavy news...I could feel it emanating from him. He straightened up from the open refrigerator door and just looked at me. "I brought something that you need to read..." He reached for the counter and handed me the e-mail, which I assumed was the origin of his burdened heart.

In moments, I, too, felt as if my feet were too heavy to lift. The reason for the message was to make us aware that it was the wish of Hannah's family that, instead of the gift of flowers to memorialize their daughter's life, the parents had requested that donations be made in her name to our ranch.

In great sorrow, honor, humility, and respect...I held the message to my chest and wept.

*Lord, hearts and lives are in pieces. Within this storm of grief... I know You have a purpose in this...even though it is hidden at this time. You have proven within my own life that out of unthinkable loss, You can raise up unthinkable purpose...unthinkable joy. Lord, let this truth find a way into the hearts of Hannah's parents, brother, and family...*

Forever faithful through sorrow and joy, the sun rose again on a brand new day.

Still feeling heavy-hearted from the night before, I was thankful that this new day dawned on what was the annual ranch "Pray Day." It's a time when staff, volunteers, family, and friends join hands and hearts together to pray over every area and horse on the ranch before the new riding season starts. After praying over the entrance, the common yard, and the hitching area, we began praying our way through the main riding herd of horses. When completed with the herd, there was one more horse to pray over—the small, gray Mustang mare that had arrived only the day before. As our group made their way into the "introduction" corral to meet and pray for the new little girl, I was still very aware that she had no name.

Suddenly interrupting my thoughts, Troy shouted over his shoulder "Wait a minute!" as he ran down the hill toward his office.

In moments, he jogged back up the hill waving a piece of paper. Still breathless, he began to read it to the group now completely surrounding the small mare. "This just came earlier," he explained, as he read a request from Hannah's parents: "I know that it is a lot to ask...I don't know if you can oblige this request or not…but would it be possible…if, in the future, when you rescue a horse…do you think you might be able to name it after our precious Hannah?"

Suddenly, my internal "stonewalling" for a name made sense. Hannah's family could not have known that the horse was already here…just waiting for a name—the *right* name. I watched in complete awe as one by one, everyone within the group raised their eyebrows in near unison, all silently asking the same question.

Finally, Chris hailed, "Hannah she *is!*" With that, everyone placed their hands on the little horse and prayed for her…by name.

———————————|·|·|———————————

In the days that followed, I learned much more about Hannah Dunn. In what I am now certain is no coincidence, Hannah's favorite car, which she loved driving, was in fact…a Mustang. In all our years of rescuing horses—more than three hundred—this was our *first rescued mustang*. Truly, it seemed so completely fitting that the car she loved to drive would also become the breed of horse that would bear her namesake.

Through contact with Hannah's parents, Randy and Melanie, a truth that has long lived within my heart was verified once again: If you see a great kid…usually, all you have to do is look over their shoulder…and you'll see great parents.

Melanie shared this: "I learned so much from her. By remembering her joy, I will endeavor to be joyful because I have life *this* day. The memory of her "mime" dance in the second grade talent show, with her vibrant, happy, full-of-life style (an image I'll never forget), still inspires me to 'give it my all.'

I can still picture her doing her homework in the old maple tree…and I determine in my heart that 'I can do all things through Christ who strengthens me.' I still picture her balancing the responsibilities of life with pleasure…and I realize that it *can* be done. Hannah was a friend to all, even those without friends. She showed me how important it is to take the time to make a difference in a person's life. It doesn't have to be big stuff; she proved that even with just a smile, a gesture, a word of encouragement…a life can be changed."

Her mother continued, "Hannah used to always say, 'Mom, if I'm gonna live, I'm gonna live BIG!' I watched her do it so often, and I now know that, for me, because of her example… the sky is the limit."

Through many tears, her father quietly summed up his relationship with his little girl by simply saying, "Maybe sometimes I treated Hannah too much like a princess…but that's only because when I thought of her as my daughter…I felt like a *king*."

Hannah Dunn lived a life of example. She was moved not only to tears by the pain of her peers…she was moved to *action*. Now, even in her loss, Hannah continues to lead by example… for those who follow her life of selfless love and choose not to be restrained by what they think they cannot do…but instead to be drawn forward by all that they *can* do.

Continuing, in part, through a little strong horse…Hannah's legacy will live on. Her namesake will carry on her newly forged tradition of loving those whom the Good Lord brings into her life here on the ranch. Hannah Dunn's selflessness of placing others first and loving them through the things that she herself loved will go forward through those who know her story…and who choose, as she did, to follow their heart.

"It is a beautiful, wonderful, mysterious mix of simplicity, innocence, and adventure that made up our Hannah Marie," her mother said. "She was our entertainment, critic, laughter, frustration, pride, and joy…she was our fireball. It is this awesome mixture that has helped me realize we don't need to be perfect in this life. (Christ has already paid that department.) Perhaps we just need to make sure that the good outweighs the imperfection in each of our believing hearts. Perhaps that is Hannah's legacy."

———————|||———————

And now, still more has happened that will serve to continue Hannah's legacy in a new and completely unexpected way.

"Hannah" the mustang is due to foal in the spring. And by the looks of all the action going on inside…true to her nickname…she's going to give birth to a real little *Fireball!*

———————|||———————

*Young Wisdom*

Nicholas, age 5, when asked to rate his first riding
experience on a scale of one to ten: "One to ten?
Hmm…I think that riding Gideon is
a ten…THOUSAND!"

# 22

## Coming Home

Since 1995 I have worked on this ranch…alone. Even though I have been surrounded by absolutely the greatest staff, volunteers, and friends a woman could ever know…my heart has carried on like a lonely soldier. Every victory, every sorrow, every shy smile, every tear, every soaring triumph, and every crushing sorrow, and all the elements that combine to create every moment of being on the ranch, has been…for me…incomplete.

From the first glimmering idea of a "ranch," until its explosion into a giant organization that has loved hundreds of horses and tens of thousands of children…there has been, within my heart, an "imbalance."

The disparity has thrived from the ranch's very beginning because Troy and I both have always had other jobs outside the ranch to help financially support it. In addition to the ranch, Troy works like a warhorse with a small team as a landscape contractor, while I work mornings, evenings, and weekends as an author and public speaker. Even though there have been "skinny" times, we have always stood on our tippy toes and reached as high as we could…trusting that God would reach toward us the rest of the way. He always did, often not in times or ways we would have chosen…but He has always been faithful to see us through

233

with just enough. Through these unique times, we have learned that enough…is as good as a feast.

With the combined work of our hands multiplied by the incredible generosity of our extended "family," the ranch continues to grow in wonderful, innovative directions. Kids, families, and horses are all being loved toward new and perhaps unexpected horizons. Each season seems to stair-step upward from the last, as we constantly learn how to better love, serve, and lead by example those who grace our ranch. All of it— every step—has been without question the greatest joy of my life. Truly, only one thing has tarnished my joy: The work Troy employs to help support the ranch…pulls him away from the very same. Because of his loving effort to help sustain the ranch, he has never really been home to experience it. The space at my side has remained empty.

For the past *eleven* years, Troy has rarely been at the ranch when the kids are present, he has never worked with a child and a horse, and he has been able to only participate in a few horse rescues.

He has quietly worked behind the scene to fix it, pay it, buck it, build it—how and whenever time allowed to get the job done.

To say that it has "not been easy" not only states the obvious but also speaks loud and clear to most working families who are attempting to do their own version of the same task. For more and more households, the unified battle cry is *"All hands on deck to keep this little boat afloat!"*

During the last eleven years, I have primarily been working the ranch as the "front man," the leader, visionary, and voice of Crystal Peaks. I have daily been involved in every joyful and difficult fiber that has become what the ranch is today. Troy has been able to experience this only from afar. I would not be honest if I didn't say that this separation from what he has worked so hard for... has created much pain in his heart.

For many years, an internal battle has raged for control of his time, effort, attention, and love. With full understanding that he could not do what his heart was calling him to do, he had to do what he *needed* to do. Many days, for many years, ended in a veil of sorrow and frustration.

The churning turmoil of emotion, desire, fatigue, and dissatisfaction all stopped one day when truth began to permeate Troy's heart. Just because we're not where *we* want to be... doesn't mean that God has abandoned us.

Truth came not because Troy "held on"; on the contrary, it came because...he let go.

The pounding waves within subsided when he changed the course of his heart from asking, "Lord, *how* can I get out of this season of pain?" to "Lord, *what* can I get out of this season of pain?"

Like a once rambunctious ox flailing about, he silently chose instead to...lean into the harness.

Everything changed. He still worked sunup to sundown as a landscape contractor; he still was not able to participate in the activities of the ranch; he still was the late-night and weekend fix-it man, bill payer, grant writer; he still wasn't "home." Yet, even so, everything was different...because *he* was different. He chose to release his grip on "*his* plan for him" and rest in *God's* plan for him.

It can be truly difficult to grow where we are planted within God's will...especially if we keep uprooting ourselves by seeking to be planted within our own will. The same can be said about how challenging a foe contentment can be—particularly when we are constantly fighting against it.

When we choose to let contentment win…*we* win too.

Peace came not when Troy got what he wanted, but when he stopped fighting, stood up straight, took a deep breath, and chose to rest in God's plan. The confession of his heart changed from "Lord, show me how to get out of landscaping and into coming home to the ranch," to "Lord, if it is Your will that I dig ditches for the rest of my life, then I will work as hard as I can to become the very best ditch digger for You…because it is now that I fully understand: It *never* was about serving me…it *always* was about serving You."

Truly, what a relief it is when we begin to comprehend that it is within our hardships that truth is elevated from our hearts…to our heads. It is our time in the desert, when we know how scorching hot the sun can really be, that we return with a new, profound appreciation of how precious cool water is. Our desert times are what grow us into who we can become. These difficult seasons force our roots to search deeper than simply how we feel, driving them down instead into what is *true*. Simply stated, if we choose, our hardships make us more appreciative, more balanced, more stable, more tenacious…

they just make us better people. Perhaps the greatest thing that our hardships make us is simply…more *ready*.

After some well-spent time in the desert, my soul mate has returned. Equipped with greater wisdom, confidence, and peace, only now is Troy ready.

Because of much faithful prayer by our ranch family both near and far, and with the continuing financial support of the same…after eleven years, God's timing has come to fruition.

As of this year…the vacancy at my side has been filled by the only one who could fill it. Now working full time at the ranch…Troy…has come home.

# EPILOGUE

## Bridge Called Hope

One of my favorite accounts in the Bible occurs when Jesus was about to feed five thousand people. Jesus, already knowing what He was planning to do, gave His disciples an opportunity to bless all those present by giving "hope" in a unique form—food.

Although the disciples had a treasurer among them who had a small amount of money, when they saw the enormity of the task—the feeding of thousands—they shrank back, completely overwhelmed. Knowing that they did not have enough resources to accomplish the task at hand, they immediately conceded defeat.

Instead of giving something...*something*...they chose instead to give nothing at all.

This recounting brings me to my knees because it makes *me* come face to face with all the moments of my own life when I was confronted with a choice—to act...or not to act. So many times, when challenged with the immensity of what rose before me...I, like the disciples, chose to do nothing at all.

Realizing that I did not have what I needed to complete the job...I chose instead...to never even start.

Thankfully, the story does not end there. Somewhere, lost within the hungry multitude, a little boy held up his hand. A *kid* came from the back and gave the disciples his lunch—five little loaves of bread and two fish. In the face of the famished masses, it wasn't very much. But it was everything he had...*and he gave it all*.

Jesus took the little boy's gift, prayed over it, and began to pass it out to everyone. Each man would break off a large-enough portion of the bread and fish to feed his family and then pass it on. Everyone ate—*everyone*—until they were completely full. When the leftovers were gathered, there was enough to fill twelve huge baskets!

In my simple way of thinking, the whole point of the story is that if we offer nothing to God...that is exactly what we can expect to happen. But if we give something—even a little thing—God can take whatever we've offered and turn it into something amazing. It is not up to me to decide *how* the Lord will use my gifts...it is only up to me to *give* them. Jesus is the One who makes the meager work of my hands into something remarkable, something effective, perhaps even something life-changing.

The truth is, if I get to *choose* my reaction to challenges...I want to choose to be like that little boy! I want to raise my hand and say, "I know that what I have isn't much...but it's all I have...and *I give it all!*"

Someone gave it all for me long ago...and my life was saved because of it. Once they decided to lay their life down as a bridge...mine was rescued the moment I *chose* to cross it.

Daily, we all have the same choice as that little boy...*all* of us.

We can each say yes...we can each make a difference in

this world by opening our hearts and *choosing* to either let hope in…or let hope out.

Like standing underneath a waterfall, hope floods our hearts. Its drenching power fills us, even the hidden parts, stretching our previous comprehension far beyond what we ever thought was possible. As we extend and grow by our continued filling and deeper understanding of hope, at some point we choose to come to a very special place. It is a place where we realize that all the sloshing fullness of hope that we have been given…is not for us to *keep*…but to *give*.

Hope is not only something we should aspire to attain…it is also something we should aspire to *give*.

It is true that every life has weights that encumber it, tying us down to only "thinking" about giving hope to those around us…instead of *actually doing it*. It is easy to become so "anchored" in focusing on our own needs that we completely overlook those within our reach who are suffering. Hope implores us to release our grip on *everything* that truly holds us back from *doing* what we know in our hearts is right. Hope is released when we begin to understand that leading others toward this "bridge" has far less to do with what we say…than with what we *do*.

Simply stated, the time has come to do more than just *feel*…we must *act*.

There is a better way, a more complete way…and it involves caring for others in need. It begins when we choose to share with them the same bridge of restoration that once healed us.

Within each heart that has ever lived…there resides a choice. It has been established by the Creator of our souls to *know* that as long as our heart beats…we have the *choice* to take action…through greatness or humility…to shoulder with the broken around us. Life has resolution when we fully understand that Hope's blade swings with perfectly balanced duality. One swing clears a path for our feet to find wholeness on the rock of Truth…the other swing cuts a hole in our hearts and like a lighthouse, allows beams of pure Truth to begin pouring out, showing others the way.

This "way" shines by virtue of our *actions*…through things as unadorned as a boy's lunch, a ranch, a cookie, or a smile.

*It is God who breathes life into our actions*, filling them with a voice that calls those who are wounded toward a very special place. It is a simple link…held out from your heart to theirs.

It is a bridge called hope.

# Bridge "Crossings"

*The Littlest Bear*—Little Bear continues to grow nearly before our eyes. Like his big buddies Luke and Boomer, his back will also be a candidate for the Christmas family photo...the *entire* family! His official education has begun and he's an eager student. Despite the severity of his childhood wounds, he bears no lingering lameness or evidence of his past other than his external scars.

*Full Circle*—Jason has been reunited with his aunt who lives in another state. He loves her very much and feels secure in the home she has opened for him. Currently he lives in close proximity to his father and is slowly building a relationship.

*Phoenix*—Phoenix continues to exemplify that we *all* can survive more than we ever thought possible. The once ugly, stinky girl that nearly starved to death has matured into a truly stunning mare. Still, to those who spend time with her, she seems to emanate the simple truth that...*life* is good.

*Cleansing Fire*—True to her character, Jenna continues to grow in humility, wisdom, grace, and beauty. She has been faithful to "stay the course" through much hardship and difficulty...while still serving others. It was with complete joy that I asked her for a small "favor." Because she truly represents the heart of what Crystal Peaks Youth Ranch is and does, Troy and I were greatly honored when she agreed to my request of being photographed with Boomer for the cover of this book.

*A Dog's Tale*—It's true that the Lord will restore the years lost. Ano continues to live in utter paradise. The dog that was once a prisoner now freely roams the foothills of the Cascade Mountains. She's not only completely adored by Mark and Kathy...but wallowed daily by their three young sons. I have seen it myself...this dog really *can* smile.

*Promise Land*—Promise has fully recovered from his hoof woes and grown into a remarkably playful young horse. He currently enjoys a wonderful home in Central Oregon where he's free to express his adventurous nature. Angelica has moved to the coast with her family, and against all odds she continues to *daily* live her life to the fullest.

*Horse with Spots*—Gideon truly *is* the little horse that could. The once battered pony who was terrified to be touched...loves his new life at Crystal Peaks.

Sarah continues to blossom in the company of "spotted love" originally forged by Shonee and now fostered by Gideon. If you ask her, Sarah will be the first to tell you: "It might not be how you think...but the Lord *does* answer prayer!"

*Coming Home*—Truly, only God can know how completely *full* my heart is...what a joy to be shoulder to shoulder and hand in hand...my Cowboy has finally come home.

*Hannah's Legacy*—Hannah came to our ranch as a small gray mustang mare that had previously been living in a garage to protect her from intentional poisoning. It was with great honor and respect that she was renamed after a courageous young woman who sought to change her world with love. Hannah Marie Dunn's legacy continues...not only through the lives of those whom she touched and the pages of this book...but also through something else— something remarkable.

I am convinced that nothing in this life is a coincidence. Hannah, our little mustang mare, delivered her foal on May 31...Memorial Day. In memory of Hannah Marie Dunn, we chose to name her beautiful, chocolate-colored filly "Hanalei," short for Hannah's Legacy. True to her legacy...she *is* a fireball!

We were first made aware of Hannah Marie's legacy by her family. Because they requested that instead of floral wreaths to memorialize their daughter, donations would be made to our ranch...I was completely overcome when I discovered later that "Hanalei" is the Hawaiian word for "wreath of flowers."

# Supporting Hope

All programs and services offered by Crystal Peaks Youth Ranch are free of charge. Nearly all the children who come to the ranch are from deeply challenging circumstances. Charges of any kind would prevent most from being able to use the ranch. Crystal Peaks Youth Ranch, therefore, is supported by individual financial gifts, grants, and fund-raising events.

It takes many strong stones to build a strong foundation. If you would like to become part of this team of dedicated supporters, please contact us by e-mail at crystalpeaks@cpyr.org or write us at the address below. Your interest in the lives of these children and their families will have a lasting impact and is deeply appreciated.

Thank you.

Crystal Peaks Youth Ranch
19344 Innes Market Road
Bend, OR 97701

*A portion of the proceeds from the sale of this book goes to support the work of Crystal Peaks Youth Ranch.*

# Where Wounded
# Spirits Run Free

STORIES FROM THE RANCH
OF RESCUED DREAMS

# Hope
# Rising

## KIM MEEDER

Kim Meeder has seen horses go where no one else can tread—stepping through the minefield of a broken child's soul in a dance of trust that only God can understand. From a mistreated horse to an emotionally starved child and back again, a torrent of love washes away their barren places. Kim's ranch is a place where this miracle happens over and over again. It is a place where the impossible flourishes, where dreams survive the inferno of reality—a place where hope rises.

You're invited to the ranch—visit crystalpeaksyouthranch.org